LIFE CHANGE

LIFE CHANGE

SIXTEEN MEN TELL THEIR EXTRAORDINARY STORIES

MARK ELSDON-DEW

First published in Great Britain in 2011 by Alpha International
Reissued in 2019 by Hodder & Stoughton
An Hachette UK company

1

A CIP catalogue record for this title is available from the British Library

Paperback ISBN 978 1 473 69423 1
eBook ISBN 978 1 473 68178 1

Typeset in Sabon MT by Hewer Text UK Ltd, Edinburgh
Printed and bound in Great Britain by Clays Ltd, Elocraf S.p.A.

Hodder & Stoughton policy is to use papers that are natural, renewable
and recyclable products and made from wood grown in sustainable
forests. The logging and manufacturing processes are expected to
conform to the environmental regulations of the country of origin.

Hodder & Stoughton Ltd
Carmelite House
50 Victoria Embankment
London EC4Y 0DZ

www.hodderfaith.com

CONTENTS

'Write down for the coming generation what the LORD has done, so that people not yet born will praise him.'

Psalm 102:18 (GNB)

INTRODUCTION

As a journalist who has been in the business a little while now, I must have interviewed thousands of people. Often I have managed to keep the human dramas involved somewhat at arm's length.

Not so with these interviews. As I have listened to the stories of these men, sometimes told with undisguised emotion, I confess I have been unable to prevent the occasional tear running down my own cheek.

There is nothing like personal real-life stories. That is why editors of popular newspapers reject articles about high-profile government initiatives, trillion-dollar business deals and even international wars in favour of a celebrity who gives a warts-and-all account of their own life.

This book contains sixteen such stories – dramatic, surprising, life-changing stories – with a special dimension: the astonishing and lasting change brought about through an encounter with Jesus Christ.

And what stories they are. Violent men suddenly work for peace, addicts overcome their addictions, convicts lead law-abiding lives and begin to offer hope to others . . .

It has not been easy for these sixteen men to speak of what has happened. On many occasions they recount past behaviour of which they are now deeply ashamed. But they have agreed to do so at my request because they long for others to know the God who changes lives.

This is the fifth in the series of books called *The God Who Changes Lives*. Most of the stories in some way involve the Alpha course, the introduction to the Christian faith now running in tens of thousands of churches of all denominations around the world. There will almost certainly be such a course running somewhere near you.

These sixteen stories bear witness to the reality of a God who loves us. As the psalmist writes, 'He brought them out of their gloom and darkness and broke their chains in pieces' (Psalm 107:14 GNB).

Mark Elsdon-Dew

1 THE STRIP-CELL PRISONER
THE STORY OF SHANE TAYLOR

For many years, Shane Taylor was considered to be one of the most dangerous prisoners in Britain's jails. Originally jailed for attempted murder, he had his sentence extended by four years when he attacked a prison officer with a broken glass in an incident that provoked a riot. After that, he was sent to some of Britain's most secure 'Category A' prisons, where he was often held in solitary confinement because of his violence towards prison officers.

My father was schizophrenic and would batter my mother. When I was a baby she escaped and fled to a battered wives' home a couple of miles from Middlesbrough. My dad would try to hunt her down. Once she moved out of the sheltered home and another woman took her room. My dad broke into the room and beat this other lady up, thinking it was my mum.

I was still a baby when mum remarried a man called Gordon Taylor and I took his name (my real name is Almond). He was like a real dad to me. When I was about six I made friends with kids who would get into trouble. I'd shoplift – pinching sweets, trainers or anything. I got caught a few times and I'd be taken home where I'd be smacked or grounded. But it didn't bother me. We did what we wanted. My mum tried everything to keep me out of trouble, but it wouldn't work.

From a very young age – eight or nine – I started going to court for burglaries, and robberies. But of course I was so young that they couldn't do anything with me except send me to foster parents or to a children's home. Then I'd just escape back home and do exactly the same things again with my friends. The police would catch me for another charge; so then I'd go back to court. It was a constant cycle.

By the time I was twelve or thirteen I was hanging around with twenty-one-year-old lads, which made me feel good. They used to do burglaries and pinch cars. All my friends stole. I didn't realise I was doing wrong at that time. By the time I knew it was wrong I couldn't stop. Sometimes my friends and I would run off and not go home for days on end. Our parents were obviously worried so they'd phone the police. The police would be out looking for us, but we would be out constantly, burgling as many places as we could. The main thing we used to do was to knock on people's doors and say, 'Excuse me, we've got to go all the way to Sunderland and we need a drink.'

And they'd go, 'Oh, you're so young. Come in while I make you a sandwich.' While they went into the kitchen, we would run into the front room and grab a purse or handbag. Then we'd run out. We used to have thousands of pounds on us from our stealing. We'd show off to our mates, going, 'Hey, do you want a tenner?' We'd end up giving half of it away. We'd go out and the older lads would buy rally cars – Astra GTs, Nova GTEs and Cosworths. Then we'd go and do other crimes in the car we'd bought. I thought, 'This is what everybody does.'

I got arrested hundreds of times, charged and taken to court. But I would get out and go straight back into it again. I had no fear. I thought, 'I'm young, I can't go to prison.'

We had these big screwdrivers to unscrew windows with, so we could get into any empty house. Once in we'd just ransack the place. There could be anything from two to five of us. We'd steal money, TVs, video machines, hi-fis, anything that would sell. We'd then take the goods straight to someone who would buy them off us. Then we'd go and do the same thing somewhere else. We'd go everywhere – Seaham, Easington, Wheatley Hill, Peterlee, Durham – wherever we could get to in the car. That was my life between the ages of nine and fourteen.

When I got caught I'd get grounded at home. To stop me running away, my stepdad nailed all the upstairs windows down. But it made no difference. I'd wait until they were in the front room before sneaking downstairs and running out.

That was when they started taking my clothes off me. So then I put my dad's clothes on and sneaked out. It was like a constant challenge for me. I knew my parents were doing these things out of love, but I didn't listen.

I went to school a bit but I ended up getting expelled from every single school. Eventually I ended up in Elemore Hall [a residential school in County Durham], which is where you go when no other school can handle you. You stay there during the week and come home at weekends. But as soon as I got there I was getting everybody to run away with me. We were pinching cars, going back home and getting together with all the lads. The police would catch us and take us back to the school. The following night I'd sneak out again.

At about thirteen or fourteen I was sent to a secure unit – Aycliffe Secure. I could have escaped if I'd really tried, but it was a nice place. There were TVs, a gym and everything. I used to get cannabis, dope and tack brought in, then my mates and I would get stoned. It was nothing like prison at all. I had a friend in prison who was writing to me, saying, 'I'm in prison. Get yourself here.' He was in Deerbolt Prison [in County Durham] and I thought, 'I want to be with all my mates.' I knew hundreds of people in there. So in order to get in there I deliberately ran away, for which I was sent to Deerbolt.

One day at Deerbolt I was bored so I got this big wooden table leg and pulled it off. Then I said to a friend, 'Do you want to start a riot?' He said 'Yeah,' so we went round saying to everyone, 'Are you up for a riot?' – and everyone was. There was a woman officer playing pool. I walked up to her, grabbed the pool balls off the table and started chucking them through the windows. Eventually we ended up in segregation and I was moved to Wetherby Prison. I was sixteen.

In Wetherby all went well until one day my pay form for working in the canteen servery arrived. It showed my payment as being £2 instead of £12, which it should have been. Soon afterwards I was putting some hot water in my cup and the officer said, 'Hurry up . . .' I held the cup up to him and said, 'I'll put this in your face.' He jumped back and I was so cross that I went back into my cell, barricaded myself in, smashed the window out, kicked the door off and waited till the riot people came. Then I walked out and went down into the 'seg'.

One day when we were in the exercise yard I said, 'Let's kick off. Let's give them trouble.' There was a metal pole bolted into the wall and I pulled it off and two of the other guys did the same. We tried to pull the barbed wire down so we could crawl up and get onto the roof. But they came in with the riot shields, screaming and shouting, got me down and handcuffed me.

Then I got moved again – this time to Moorland Prison [near Doncaster]. I was on the wing for dangerous young offenders. I kept my head down and eventually got released from there. But by now I'd started to get violent – I'd fight anybody and was up for anything. I had this motto: 'If you want to survive in a criminal world you've got to become more violent than the violent.' So my aim was to instil fear in people. I would go after whoever I felt like. If I couldn't find him, I would go after somebody else in his family. I wanted to be so feared that people would fear the fact that I was walking near them. I didn't have any morals like some criminals have.

From the age of fourteen or fifteen I'd carried a knife. I had a fascination with guns and knives – mainly knives.

They were like a god to me. Having a knife in my hand was like the thing. They'd be big, ten-inch, kitchen blade knives. If anyone came up to me or I felt threatened, I'd pull it out and use it. Eventually I had a whole set of knives strapped round my waist – the smaller one up to the bigger one. One time one of my knives led to me being set up by the police. They had caught me stealing a car and cornered me in a back garden. That was where they said that I pulled a knife out on them. But it was a set-up. I had the knife on me, but the policeman pulled the knife out and said that I pulled it out on him. So I started thinking, 'He set me up. I hate him.' In the interview they asked, 'So, why did you pull a knife out on the police officer?'

I said, 'I wish I did and I wish I'd killed him.'

And they said, 'You don't mean that, do you?'

I said, 'I do mean it. Before I die I'm going to kill a police officer or somebody who has anything to do with authority.' I got to the point where I felt no fear.

One time in prison there were these black lads from London. In the exercise yard they were challenging people and fighting with them. When they came to me I just ran at them, swung a few punches and went mad. Then the prison officers came running out and put a stop to it. The next day I walked past these black lads and smashed my dinner plate over one of them. The dinner went everywhere and we started battling on the floor. I later found out this lad was well known in the London area for being pretty hard. Another time I went to the door of a man (who thought he was the main man) and asked him if he knew if the mail had been given out. He went, '**** off!' I was so mad. I went into my cell and stormed up and down, getting madder and madder and shouting to my cellmate, 'I'm gonna kill him!' I walked out the door and saw this guy walking down the stairs. I went up to him and said, 'Tell me to **** off, did you?'

He went, 'Yeah, I did. Why? Have you got a problem?' Before he could finish I smacked him in the face and he went flying into the doorway. Then I started punching him and leathering him. Six or seven prison officers appeared and tried to get me off him but they couldn't. I carried on hitting him, shouting, 'I'm gonna kill you!' That's when one of the prison officers punched me and I let go and fell on the floor. I got put in segregation again for that. By the time I got out of that prison, I was getting into a bit of drugs and more violence.

I went to Hartlepool where there was a local hard man, well known by everybody. People said, 'He's a feared man. No one will dare touch him.' He was a really big, powerful, mentally ill person. He had taken a video machine from two young lads I knew. This hard man had heard they were trying to sell it and had pulled out a hammer on them and taken it. So we went after him. One lad had a big aluminium baseball bat, the other had a knife – and I had a nine-inch knife.

When we approached him he said, 'Come on . . .' One lad ran at him and was whacking him with the bat. I thought, 'I need to help him here, he's only young.' So I ran at the hard man and stabbed him. As I was doing it he hit me with the hammer. I can remember seeing sparks and then I can't remember anything else. When I came back round I was a mile away from the scene, running away with these two lads. I thought I still had the knife in my hand, but I only had the knife handle.

I looked at the lads and they were white. I said, 'What's happened?' They said, 'You've killed him. You stabbed him through his head, Shane. He's pouring with blood.' I said, 'Have I?' Then we ran all the way back to Peterlee. It turned out he was a very hard man. The knife had gone right through the top of his head and come out above his eye. He pulled the knife out with his own hand and vowed that he would get me back. It was all over the news. I got caught and they tried to charge me with the offence, but in the end it got dropped and they charged me with affray.

Some time after that I stabbed a local hard man in the shoulder while we were in a pub. The police were informed, so I was on the run.

I then 'taxed' (robbed) a fifteen-year-old drug dealer because I needed the money. When I finally got caught, the charge was Section 20 – GBH. I was nineteen. I got Section 20 for the two stabbings, a couple of affrays and carrying offensive weapons. I was sentenced to four years. At first I was in Northallerton but then, when I turned twenty-one, I was sent to Holme House Prison in Stockton-on-Tees.

A lot of people had heard about me before I got to Holme House. I was crazy, doing loads of violent and mad things. People would say things like, 'There's Shane over there. He's off his head, don't mess with him.' There was a lad in Holme House who used to bully me when we were kids. He came up to me and said, 'Can you remember that time when I nutted you? I'm so sorry, I didn't mean to do it . . .'

I loved the attention I was getting. It made me feel like a king. I was the madman that everyone looked up to – and I had a gang of people who would do what I asked them to do.

One time I set up this prisoner who I needed to get. I got him down into the gym, punched him and smashed his eye open. Another time a prison officer refused to let me out of our wing so that I could go to the gym (after originally saying that he would let me go). So I said, 'How come you never let me out?' He went, 'What a pity.' So I went, 'You're dead – you're going to get it . . .' I was swearing and getting angry. And he said, 'Oh, how many times have I heard that?'

Then I went up to this little lad who was playing pool and said, 'Pick up them pool balls and chuck them at that screw.' He went 'Oh . . .' I said, 'Do you want a name for yourself? Do you want people to know you? Do you want my respect?' He went, 'Yeah.' I said, 'Then just do it.' So he picked up the pool balls and started chucking them at this prison officer. The officer came running towards us and pulled out his baton.

I was holding a large coffee jar and I smashed the end of it and held the broken glass in my hand. As he approached me he tried to boot the glass out of my hand and then I stabbed him three times – first on his arm, then in his legs. I was in a frenzy now – my mind was blank and I was going mad. While all this was happening the other inmates were chucking pool balls at the officers – it nearly led to a big riot. While I was restrained, the officer that I'd stabbed picked up my hand and squashed it down onto the jagged edges of the coffee jar. After that I was sentenced to another four years on top of my original sentence. I was sent to Durham Prison and put in segregation. (When you attack prison officers you're classed as highly dangerous.)

While I was there, one of the prison officers came to me and said provocatively, 'Aaah, you haven't got any weapons now . . .' On the ceiling of my cell were these long lights. At the end they've got big metal things, but in prison they're put in with a certain screw so they cannot be screwed out. But I knew how to get them out. I got one out – this big, heavy, metal thing. Then I went to the door, holding it up. About four officers all dived back when they saw me. I said, 'Here, come and get it!' They all looked at each other. Then one of them came over, dead slow, with his hand out, and took it off me. And I said to the one who had been provocative with me, 'Next time you say that, I will cave your skull in. This is just a warning – don't wind me up.' Then I walked back into my cell and shut the door.

After that, I was sent to a maximum security prison – Frankland Prison. They put me straight into the segregation unit. They felt I was a danger to everybody. A maximum-security prison is designed for dangerous prisoners. Then you've got the segregation unit inside that for the really uncontrollable. Then, inside the segregation unit, you've got the CSC [Close Supervision Centre] where prisoners are so dangerous that there can be no physical contact between them and the prison officers.

To begin with I was all right in normal segregation. But after a while I felt the officers were winding me up, so I started kicking off and battling with them. They'd come with their riot gear and fight me. I shouted at them, 'When

I get a chance, you're a dead man. I want to stab you.' They couldn't take the chance – I'd already stabbed a prison officer – so they put me in Close Supervision.

At the bottom of your cell door you've got a hatch through which you get a big metal square box that they put your food in. You're not allowed out of your cell and there's no physical contact. My door couldn't be opened unless there were six to seven prison officers with riot shields and riot gear. For my exercise they'd handcuff me and take me into this little caged exercise yard. They'd take my handcuffs off, then leave me in this cage. I was in the CSC for about a year.

The officers that work in the seg get bored, so they try and wind you up – physically and mentally. As a result of this I'd end up smashing the toilets. Then I'd get put in a strip cell. They take all your clothes and put you in a little box with no window. It's dark and freezing cold and there's nothing in there but a little cardboard thing to wee and poo in. You're too cold to sleep, so you just curl up into a ball. You are put in these strip cells for as long as you choose to be. It's like a burning-off thing to calm you down. If you're still kicking off in there, then they leave you there for a few days.

I did these kinds of things in a whole lot of different prisons. Eventually, when I was about twenty-six, I got moved into Parkhurst on the Isle of Wight. I'd been in prison since I was nineteen. This time, instead of taking me to the seg as they would usually do, they said, 'We're going to give you a chance.' The prison officer said to me, 'Look, we'll be sound with you if you'll be sound with us.' I respected that and I was sound with them.

I ended up selling drugs in the prison (smack, etc.) and making a bit of money every now and then. A few months later I met a lad called Robert Bull. He was in prison for murder, but since getting inside he'd become a born-again Christian. He was saying a load of things that sounded mad to me. But the one thing that stuck in my mind was when he said this: 'I've been in prison for fifteen years and am probably never getting out – but I'm free.' I used to think, 'What's he on about? How can he be free if he's never getting out?' He was on the same wing as me and he kept coming to me and giving me little booklets like *Why Jesus?* by Nicky Gumbel. I used to chuck them on the side but every now and then, when I was bored, I'd pick up the booklet and read through it. I thought nothing of it.

I began to realise that fighting the system by violence only made me lose because I ended up staying in jail for a longer time. That way, I'd never get out. But I didn't want the system to win so I thought the way to beat it without them getting me was to 'disturb' the place. So with my drugs money I started paying people to set the riot alarm off. As soon as it went off, the officers would all come running. Then a couple of minutes later another riot bell would be set off in another part of the prison. This disturbed the prison in a big way and I knew it was upsetting them – they were getting mad. Then I started paying others to set bins and cells on fire. Soon the prison was chaos.

They eventually sensed that I was behind it all. They called me into the office and threatened to bang me up for a couple of days. So I said, 'That's only going to make

people even angrier – great, that'll just start a riot!'
Eventually I got put in seg – they said it was because of my
'subversive behaviour'. They knew I was smuggling drugs
and they knew I was using some kind of power to over-
throw the prison system – or at least to disturb it. When I
was in seg I went on a dirty protest. I smashed the front
window out in the door and stayed on a dirty protest for a
couple of days. Then I relaxed, chilled out and they gave
me a TV – I was still in seg. I think they gave me a TV
because they know that once they give you things, you don't
want to lose them, so you start being good.

As I was sat there in my cell I got a big vision of that
Christian prisoner, Robert Bull, and an urge telling me to
write him a letter. The urge was so strong that I got up and
walked up and down my cell, talking out loud to myself,
'How can I write to him? I don't even know who he is.' This
urge remained in my head for three or four days. Eventually
I wrote this letter to him (he was in the normal wing),
saying, 'Look, I don't know why, but I've got a strong urge
telling me to write you a letter and a vision of you in my
head, so I'm writing to you . . .'

He wrote back, 'The Lord's trying to open your eyes, to
get to your heart. Just let go.' I thought, 'He's crazy,' but I
continued writing to him. I even started to read the
Gideon's Bible in my cell a little. I was segregated and
there was nothing much to do. Four months later they
moved me to a maximum-security prison at Long Lartin
in Worcestershire.

I got to Long Lartin and walked onto the wing towards
my cell – and there, standing right outside my door, was a

church minister. I said to him, 'For some reason I've been reading the Bible.' He went, 'Have you? Have you heard of the Alpha course? Why don't you go on it?' I'd never heard of the Alpha course but I said, 'Yeah, put my name down' – and thought nothing of it at all.

A few months later my door opened and I was told to go to the education department. So I went. I walked in and sat down and discovered it was the Alpha course. A lady asked me my name and I said Shane.

She said, 'Are you meant to be here?'

I went, 'Don't know.'

She said, 'Well, your name's not down. Do you want to stay?'

All the lads there were saying, 'Shane, you get free chocolate biscuits, gateau and coffee.'

So I said, 'Yeah, get my name down.' My intention wasn't to find God. I was thinking, 'Free coffee, chocolate biscuits and gateau!' I settled down quite quickly and began to turn up to each of the sessions. For each session we had a talk on video with Nicky Gumbel preaching. But I was mostly interested in getting the chocolate biscuits and having little debates, saying things like, 'Science proves that it's wrong . . .'

Eventually we got to the Holy Spirit day. After we'd watched the videos and had our discussion, everyone sat down and we each got prayed for. The minister Eddie Baker put his hand on my head and prayed for me but nothing particularly happened.

Later on I was making a cup of coffee when he came up to me and said, 'I've never done this in all the years I've worked here, but I think God is telling me to tell you to come back here this afternoon.'

I said, 'All right then, I'll come.' I remember saying to myself, 'If it's real then prove it.' I went to the church that afternoon and Eddie was there waiting for me. He picked up a Bible and opened up a few verses where it said something like, 'Jesus Christ died on a cross for you. He died for your sins and you can be forgiven.'

Then Eddie put his hand on my head and prayed for me. Then he took his hand off and said, 'Now you pray.'

I said, 'What about?'

And he said, 'From your heart – let it out and pray.'

I said, 'Jesus Christ, I know you died on a cross for me. Please, I don't like who I am, please forgive me, please.' I said a few other things, which I can't remember now. And then I sat back and we started talking. As I talked I started to feel a weird feeling in my belly. I thought, 'What's that?' But I kept talking to him. Then I started to feel this bubbly feeling slowly coming up my body – through my legs, my chest. When it got to about halfway I started to feel tears coming into my eyes.

I tried to hold it back. I stopped talking, thinking that was going to stop it, because I didn't want to cry. Here I was, a hard man in prison – I didn't want to cry. But it rose up and up and up until suddenly I began crying my eyes out. I hadn't cried in years. I cried for about five minutes and I could feel a weight being lifted off me because I felt light. Eddie said in a nice voice, 'That's the Holy Spirit. It's Jesus.'

I looked up and said, 'Don't tell anyone I've been crying.'

And he went, 'If it's God's will, you'll be telling them.'

I felt like I was in this room where although there was natural light, somebody had switched on another light and everything suddenly became clearer than before. It felt as if I'd had an invisible layer covering my eyes and it was rubbed away. In that split second I knew it was real. I knew God existed, I knew Jesus had touched me and that I was going to live for him forever.

The first thing I did after that was to go back to the wing and run into my friend's cell. He was sat eating his meal. I said, 'I've been crying. Jesus is real. He's just come to me. He's real!'

He thought I was mad and chucked me out of his cell. I ran up to these prison officers and said, 'It's real!' They looked at each other and said, 'What's real?'

I was going, 'Jesus Christ is real!' And they were like, 'All right, then, see you later.'

Everything changed overnight. My behaviour changed so much that I went from being in the segregation to getting a trusted job in the chaplaincy within a few weeks.

Within months I ended up on the enhanced wing, which is where you get extra privileges for good behaviour. My behaviour changed – if I was challenged, I was like, 'Oh it's all right, no problem.' The prison officers were definitely sceptical of a man like me suddenly changing his ways – so they used to challenge me. One day I was sat on the wing and two or three prison officers came down and one of them said to me, 'Jesus Christ, he's a ****ing this, he's a ****ing that . . .' swearing and swearing. I stood there for a bit and let him say it. Then I turned round, pointed at him and said, 'Would you have spoken to me like that a few months back?' He put a face on as if to go, 'Phwaor, no!' I went, 'Well, that proves the change, doesn't it?' And I walked into my cell.

That was definitely the Holy Spirit giving me that answer – it didn't come from me. Later when I went round the office to get something, the woman officer who was there came up to me, shook my hand and went, 'Well done. I can't believe how you reacted to that. Keep it up!' So I started getting praises off the officers – I couldn't believe it. I no longer saw the officers as representatives of 'the system' – I started to see that they were just human beings who make mistakes, like I have. I started talking to them, having full-scale conversations about God with them. The officers began to see that I was doing the right things. I started sending money to this charity in Africa. I prayed constantly. I used to pray to get the gift of tongues, which I got, and I prayed for the officers and for my enemies.

Not long after all this, I was lying on my bed in my cell. All the bad things I'd done to people flicked through my head and all the times I'd upset people – and I started crying. I realised that for many years I'd been aggressive towards people without even realising it.

There was an Islamic man in the prison who was suspected of being a police informer. That is very danger- ous in a maximum-security prison. One day when we were out on exercise I walked straight up to him and said, 'All right, mate?'

He went, 'You do know, don't you?'

'What?'

He said, 'You don't need to walk around with me. You know your life's in danger, don't you?'

'No, why?'

He went, 'Because they think I'm an informer, so if they're going to come after me, they'll come after whoever's with me. That's why I'm all on my own. You don't want to be around me.'

The exact words I said to him were, 'I don't fear man. I love Jesus Christ and I know he's with me.' We talked away and I said to him at the end, 'God's going to deal with this. Jesus is going to sort this out.'

He went, 'How do you know?'

I said, 'Because I'm going to pray.'

After that, I prayed every night, 'Father, let them forget about it and let them be his friend again.' A week later he came running into my cell and said, 'Nothing's happened, Shane.' I had so much faith in this prayer I said, 'Don't worry, trust me. I promise you Jesus is going to sort it out. Just go.' And he walked off.

I kept praying and about four days later he came running in and went, 'I don't believe it!' I went, 'What?'

He said, 'It's as if they've forgotten about it. They all just suddenly started talking to me again. It's as if it never happened.'

And I went to him, 'Can I tell you what I've been praying for now? I prayed that they would just forget about it.'

And he was like, 'Whoa . . .!'

By this stage I was reading the Bible loads and going to chapel every Sunday. The only reason I'd ever been to chapel before had been to pass a few drugs to somebody. I also helped on some Alpha courses with Eddie – and I did a basic Bible study course in prison, using tapes.

After I'd been a Christian for a while, a lad came to me and pulled a knife out on me. I flipped and tried to grab him and said, 'I'm going to do you!' But then I went into my cell, shut the door, dropped to my knees and said, 'God, please forgive me, I didn't mean to do it. Please forgive me.' It broke me, so I went to Eddie and said, 'How have I changed? I've still committed violence.'

And he said, 'Two years ago what would have happened to that person?'

I said, 'I would definitely have seriously hurt him.'

'And what did you do this time?'

I said, 'I dropped to my knees and asked God to forgive me.'

Then I realised I'd changed. From then on it got better and better. I prayed to God that he would enable me to meet the man that I'd stabbed in the head, so that we could sort it out. He ended up in the same segregation, a couple of doors away from me. He came to the window and said, 'Shane, let's just forget it.' God made that happen – that's not human nature. If somebody stabs you, especially in the criminal world, your instinct is for revenge, no matter how long it takes.

Almost exactly a year after the Holy Spirit day that changed my life, I was freed. Not long before I got out of prison I went before a board where there was a governor, probation and all that. They asked me, 'So do you think you'll go back to prison?'

I said, 'No, I'm not going back to prison.'

They said, 'Why?'

I was so on fire for God I said, 'Because the Lord Jesus Christ's touched me, I'm telling you it's real . . . I know I'm not coming back to prison because God is with me.'

When I went out Eddie the minister said to me, 'You're not even out yet and God's already using you.'

I got out in May 2007. My mum and my Auntie Cath were there to meet me. I'd been writing massive letters to my mum, saying things like, 'The Lord's touched me . . .' When I got out my mum said to me, 'I think it's just a put-on. Now you're out you'll go back to what you normally do.'

But I didn't. Immediately after coming out of prison I started going to church at the One Life Church. It's a free church. The first time I went I knew it was the right church for me. I go every Sunday. I've helped on some of their Alpha courses. I was struggling to find a job. So I prayed to God, 'Look, God, I need a job, because if I don't I'm going to end up going back to my old life . . .' I was struggling with everything. A couple of days later a woman who'd recently moved in over the road came to the front door and said, 'I'm a manager at Monitor [a local store] – could your son work for us?' So I ended up getting a job there.

About seven months later I met Sam. Sam used to be a real rebel – she took coke and did criminal acts. I ended up going out with her and I fell from God a bit. Eventually I started talking to her about Jesus and saying, 'Why don't you come to church?' She finally did come. During the service a woman got up and said, 'I woke up at 4 am and was told to say that there's somebody here who's suffered . . .' and she named some things. Every single thing she said related to what had happened to Sam. Her life totally changed after that – she became a Christian and our relationship continued to grow. That put me properly back with God again.

We got married on 11 October 2008 at South Bank Baptist Church. There were over 100 people there. We weren't allowed more because of the fire regulations. Eddie preached during the service. It was an amazing day – I cried my eyes out. Everyone did.

Jesus has changed my life. He's changed me beyond belief – almost as if it's not me. Now I could stand in front of a criminal who's committed a bad offence and love them. I don't care what anybody's done. I couldn't have done that before. Jesus has showed me how to love and how to forgive. I talk to him on a daily basis; I speak to him as if I'm having a normal conversation. I see him do things in front of my eyes that I've prayed for. Before I was a man of pure hate and anger. I blamed the world. Everything was always the world's fault or the system's fault. Now I realise it's not the world's fault.

Since becoming a Christian I've never committed a criminal offence – never pinched a car, never burgled a house and never stolen. I did struggle with a bit of anger, but that has gone. I used to swear constantly but not now. A lot of things changed in me. I wanted to make peace with the man I'd stabbed through the shoulder. He didn't believe that I'd found God so I spoke to someone he knew and said, 'I'm not the same person. I want to shake that man's hand.' He came to the pub, shook my hand and said, 'It takes a man to do what you've just done. Thanks.' And that was that. That is God.

Almost all the people I've upset, all the people I stabbed, all the people I hurt have forgiven me and now we talk. The only one thing that I hope and pray for occasionally is for the prison officer that I stabbed. I've written to him, asking him to forgive me for what I did. At this time he doesn't want to have anything to do with me – and I can understand that. But one day . . .

I thank Jesus for coming to Nicky Gumbel and helping him set up the Alpha courses, because otherwise people like me wouldn't get the chance to hear about God.

Now I'm helping with Alpha courses in prisons. It's a miracle that I'm allowed to go visiting prisons when I've just been released from a maximum-security prison. Now I'm able to tell other prisoners about Jesus – it's amazing.

My mum texted me recently, saying, 'Even though I don't believe in God, I thank him for taking you out of the grasp of the devil.' Another text she sent made me cry. It said, 'I am so proud of you . . . You're the best son ever.'

Jesus has saved me. He's forgiven me for what I've done. He's changed my life around. It says in the Bible he came to give 'fullness of life'. He's giving me things that I never thought I'd have.

Shane Taylor and his wife Sam now have five children. They attend a local church. Shane says, 'I never believed God would give me a lovely family. God is great.'

2 'THE WALRUS OF ARSENAL' THE STORY OF SIMON PINCHBECK

As a policeman, Simon Pinchbeck took part in 'horren-dous battles' with football thugs and came to be known as 'The Walrus of Arsenal'. Then, several years later, he met one of the hooligans he'd chased and found him a changed man. The man invited him to church . . .

Family life was pretty difficult when I was growing up. My 'father' – the man who brought me up – wasn't my natural father and came into my life when I was about four. I never knew my natural father. I was an illegitimate son.

Up until the age of four, we lived with my grandparents, who spoiled me, and life was lovely. Then, all of a sudden, life completely changed. My new father was a young guy who wanted to stamp his authority on me from an early age and he would shout at me and smack me. I had never been hit before in my life. I will never forget the things he did to me.

As I grew up, I became known as someone who could have a fight if need be. I don't think I was a nasty sort of guy but I wasn't someone anyone would mess with and I didn't have any hassle at school. When I was about fifteen or sixteen, I started running with a group of football hooligans. We would all go on the train to Derby's away games and the train would get wrecked, absolutely smashed up.

We'd smash the tables and rip the seats and everyone thought it was great fun. Light bulbs would be thrown on the platform at the other fans. At the ground, there would be fighting before, during and after the game. I enjoyed the adrenaline rush.

When I left school I didn't have a clue what I was going to do. I wanted to make some money but I didn't really know how. I worked in a brewery for a while and my alcohol threshold was phenomenal. People were amazed at the amount of beer I could drink in the bar at night, which gave me some sort of kudos. Drink was part of the culture. I was very big into the macho image and thought, 'I'll join something with a bit of street cred. I'll join the Metropolitan Police.' So I did. That was August 1976 and I was nearly nineteen. The training lasted sixteen weeks.

After passing out of college, I realised there were certain things I had to do in the police force to fit in. The more macho you were, the more people talked about you and held you in esteem, and the more people patted you on the back.

I was a big guy and if there were a couple of people who had been arrested and weren't saying the right things, then they'd use me to intimidate them. It was part of the job and you had to do that to fit in. Taping police interviews didn't come in until about 1984–85.

People would say about me, 'He's all right to work with, he's as good as gold,' which meant that he doesn't mind writing whatever needs to be written to get the conviction.

I was at Holloway from 1976 until 1987. I was never anything more than a PC but the duties I did were really varied. You would deal with the old dear who had been mugged; you'd deal with the person who'd been burgled; the fighting; the robberies; the street crime; every aspect of street policing. As a policeman at Holloway, our force was responsible for crowd control at the Arsenal football ground.

I made a reputation for myself there as someone who didn't mind getting stuck into the aggro. I had a big moustache in those days and they called me 'the Walrus'. They always looked on me as 'their' Old Bill, 'their' police. Even to this day I can go to places and people will go, 'All right mate, want a drink?'

I met my wife, Linda, when I was twenty-four or twenty-five. Her father was a police inspector and we sort of bumped into each other in the road and got a conversation going. We were married in a Catholic church, which I wanted to do for my Gran, who was a very devout Catholic. At first, married life was quite difficult. My wife was very close to her mother, and her dad, despite being a police inspector, was an alcoholic.

Obviously the mother looked to the support of the daughter and the daughter was getting pulled both ways. It was hard for her but I couldn't see that at the time. It made things a bit tense.

What with the macho thing, I thought I could live the single life within the confines of a marriage. I couldn't have been that easy to live with and I'm sure she knew I had the odd fling but she would just choose to ignore it. She never challenged me.

It was a good four or five years of my life. I was big, I was strong, I was fit. I did the boxing and people thought I was a great person, and I was totally respected. In 1984 I won the police heavyweight boxing championship, which only added to my reputation. That same year, we had our first child, a boy. Our second, another boy, was born in 1986. They were christened because I had my granny in the back of my head.

Some time after that, I joined a unit called the Territorial Support Group (TSG). We were based at Paddington and were trained to be fitter than the average policeman. We'd be used to take out people with knives, riots or even house-to-house enquiries on big murder investigations – all sorts of serious things.

We worked very closely with the Football Intelligence Unit at Scotland Yard. For a couple of years whenever there was a football match and we thought there would be trouble I'd be there. We had informants in every single hooligan group except Millwall. Money talks and the informants would cop their few hundred quid and then start ratting on all their friends. So we appeared wherever there'd be trouble. I've been in some horrendous battles at Arsenal and Millwall.

I got so into this football thing, it sort of possessed me a bit. While it was going on I wasn't at home and I neglected my wife. In 1994 I discovered that my wife had been confiding in another fellow. She said it was nothing more than someone to confide in, but I found out who it was and went round and threatened him. He was someone she was working with. We got through that.

I was with the TSG for four or five years. Then I moved to Enfield, where I did ordinary beat duty, patrolling the streets in plain clothes. I've always had a good eye for someone to stop. I would say, 'Let's stop him over there.' And we'd stop him and he'd have drugs on him or a knife or something – it was just experience.

At that time I got involved with a girl much younger than me. I had reached forty and went right off the rails really. I started drinking heavily and taking drugs. I started going to clubs and didn't care what my wife thought.

By now I was a bit of a dinosaur in the police force as things were changing. There were still some people operating the way I did, but the old days were changing. It was more computerised.

I started leading two lives – one with my wife and one trying to see this other girl. I ended up getting into such a mess with everything that I went to see my doctor and he put me on anti-depressants. In November 1997, I left home for three months. I was so mixed up, I just didn't know what was happening. I didn't even care much about my children at that time. A friend of mine was on a round-the-world trip and so I stayed in his place. That did a lot of damage to the kids and it was a good couple of years before they trusted me again.

Around this time I met a couple of criminals at my gym. I knew they were slippery but I didn't know how slippery they were. I used to go running with one of them in the mornings and we'd have a chat when we were running. He introduced me to some celebrities and I went on a bit of a celebrity kick and all that.

He was on these steroids and said, 'Have a go at them.'

I said, 'Yeah, OK.' I bought a course and began injecting them in my bum. They made me stronger but a bit more aggressive.

At the beginning of July 1998 – by this time I was so messed up – I went to a club. At the end of the evening I went over to say goodbye to a girl I knew on the dance floor and suddenly something snapped inside me and I ended up hitting some bloke. I gave him a right good whack. I knocked his tooth out and he fell to the floor, bang, crash. It turned out he was an off-duty policeman. I then just walked out. I knew all the bouncers because I used to work in there under cover. The skin on my hand was hanging off and I ended up going to the hospital. I rang my wife and told her I'd fallen over.

Next day, a policeman friend came to pick me up to go to work and he said to me, 'You're in a bit of trouble. The fellow has been told to press charges.' I went into work and immediately got suspended from duty. It was quite a low point.

My hand blew up out of all proportion. When the hospital had sewed the skin on my hand together, the wound had got infected and the doctors became worried about septi-caemia. Meanwhile, I didn't quite know what was going to happen. I got myself a solicitor and my defence obviously rested on reports from my doctor and a psychiatrist. If I was found guilty I would be sent to prison.

I ended up going to Woolwich Crown Court and spent a week in the box down there. I think I lost about two or three stone during the whole week. In the end, I got acquitted on medical grounds based on the reports from my doctor and psychiatrist.

I was then asked whether I wanted to go back in the police force or not, but by that time I had cooked my own goose. I had had so many psychiatric reports done on me that I couldn't really go back in.

So I said, 'No, I'll call it a day.' I got medically discharged in February 2000.

While I was in the police force I had taken out an insurance policy which kept my wages up if I got medically discharged, so that I could just about survive on the money.

But soon after leaving the police, I met a fellow at a local gym and I spent about eighteen months doing a few slippery things with him earning a bit of cash. I thought, 'This is it. This is easy street. This is what I was meant to do.' Along with the money from that and the money from my pension, I was living very nicely. I thought, 'Yeah, I can't see this ending.' Then I got taken for a ride by one of the other fellows at the gym. I put some money into something that went pear-shaped and I lost the money. I had foolishly trusted this guy. It was my own fault and I deserved everything I got.

Then another fellow came along and set up something and I was taken to the cleaners again. But I had no comeback. What could I say? I couldn't say anything. If I'd started on them, it would have been a war that I couldn't win. After the second time I said, 'Look, I know what's going on here. You've carved me up and I don't want to see you again.' In the criminal world there is no honour amongst thieves. People will do anything for money. I lost about £20,000 the first time and £35,000 the second time.

At the gym I met up with a boxer who had a friend who had been a right villain in the past, but whose life had been turned around when he became a Christian. I knew of him in the police and through reputation. He was part of a nasty crowd. I knew of him through the football as well because he was a football hooligan at one time, but that didn't twig until later.

Physically I was looking fantastic but mentally and spiritually there was nothing there whatsoever. I just looked at him and I thought, 'There is something there.' He seemed to have such a sense of inner peace within himself. He would tell me about the work he was doing in prisons and I said, 'Can I spend a bit more time with you?' He said, 'Yeah, we'll have chats.' His name was Bryn. I remember going up to the gym one day and he was there and he was so full of life, with such a big smile on his face.

One day he said, 'Meet me for lunch.' So I met him for lunch and he brought another fellow along. We had a chat and he said, 'You're searching for something.'

I said, 'Yes, I've been searching for something for ages.'

He said, 'Come to my church.'

I thought of churches as a structured thing with services and ranting the prayers off. I had been involved in churches because of the kids. I got them into an ecumenical school near me and you had to be pretty active in your church, so as a means to an end I'd run a youth club and done all sorts of things. But I fell out with the priest.

Bryn took me to Holy Trinity Brompton. I walked through the door and there was just so much power, so much love, and I thought, 'I'm home here.' The service was so brilliant. I thought, 'They're speaking to you about the Word of God here and it actually makes sense. It's not a rant or anything. It's actually stuff that makes sense.' Nicky Gumbel got up and talked and I thought, 'This is brilliant.' I'd never seen anything like that in my life before.

People were greeting me and shaking my hand. Being a policeman you're a bit cynical and I thought, 'What's he after?' But you soon realised that these were genuinely good people. I was sitting down with Bryn and he said to me, 'Do you know Nicky Gumbel?'

I said, 'No, I've never heard of him before. Who is this fellow?'

He then got Nicky, who came and sat down next to me. He asked if I wanted to be a Christian and if I wanted to turn away from everything I knew was wrong. I said I did, so I prayed that with him.

After that I kept in contact with Bryn and kept coming back to Holy Trinity. I couldn't go every week because of the distance but I visited when I could. In the meantime I found out that Bryn had been on the terraces as a football hooligan and I used to chase him around when I was a copper. He was an Arsenal fan.

We were sitting down at a table once and I said, 'Yeah, I did a lot of football over at Arsenal. Lots of people used to call me "the Walrus".'

'No, you're not the Walrus.'

I said, 'Yeah, I was.' And we went on and on: 'Do you remember this? Do you remember that?'

I said to him about Christianity, 'I really feel this is for me.'

He said, 'Well, the next thing you've got to do is Alpha.'

'What's that about?'

'Oh, it's just about examining your faith and the meaning of life and stuff like that.' He didn't give me any leaflets to read but he gave me a couple of 'tough guy' sort of books about villains, and stuff that had turned their life around through Christ. He showed me a video of Paul Cowley. I thought that was fine but it was the change that this fellow Bryn had gone through that really got me going. So I rang up the Alpha office at Holy Trinity and there was a course starting in May (this was 2002), and I got myself onto that course.

I went along to the first evening and there were hundreds of people and they had a big tent outside the church. There was then a massive dinner and I thought, 'Cor, I didn't think there were going to be so many people.'

I sat there and then Nicky Gumbel gave an introduction. The first talk was 'Who is Jesus?' and it really hit the spot. I sat there in awe of what he was saying.

In my discussion group they were all slightly older than me. They'd come from different walks of life although none of them had experienced the sort of street life that I had. I found myself saying things and thinking, 'Where's this come from?'

I couldn't wait to get to the next Wednesday. Before each evening I got out Nicky Gumbel's book about the Alpha course, *Questions of Life*, and I'd read through the topic. I'd either read it through at home or I'd arrive a bit early, have a cup of coffee across the road and read the book.

I'd think, 'Yeah, this is what it is all about. This is what life's about. This is it.'

The leaders of our group were good. We had a few people with opinions in the group and they would try and steer it. I was in a little bit of trepidation about the weekend away. I didn't know what to expect but people kept saying, 'Oh, you'll love it, you'll get so much from it.' I thought, 'Well, I should go to it.'

On the Sunday of the weekend I had been invited to play rugby at Twickenham. I coached an under-18s rugby team and one of the dads works for Carlsberg Tetley and they were having a corporate day. There were twelve teams and he said, 'Would you help me come along and run it and will you play?'

First of all when he said it, I said, 'No, I'm going on an Alpha weekend.' He goes to church and so he knew what I meant and said, 'OK, I understand.' I then spoke to the leaders and I said, 'What's the main day on the Alpha weekend?'

They said, 'The Saturday.'

So I said to my mate, 'OK, John. I'll come on the Sunday, I'll come straight to the rugby.'

The Alpha weekend was held at Pakefield in Suffolk. The Friday night and the Saturday were so brilliant. I've been away on weekends before, mostly stag weekends, and it's normally full of drinking and debauchery and whatever. But at this weekend, there were lots of young people and they were so full of love and goodness and stuff.

On the Saturday afternoon, Nicky spoke and then said, 'If you want to close your eyes I'm going to ask the Holy Spirit to come.' I wasn't too sure what he was on about but I'd learned through the course to trust and open myself up, to drop down the barriers and to let whatever was going to happen, happen. I stood there with my eyes closed and I felt an incredible feeling. I felt the Holy Spirit inside me. It was a feeling of fullness – no worries. I was on a different plane.

A couple of my leaders came and prayed with me, which was really fantastic. I asked them to pray for me to be strong. There are areas of my life, like everybody has, that I'm weak in. Women is one area – but there are lots of others. So they prayed that I'd be strong. That night, I went back home and on the drive back I felt I was on a cloud. It was brilliant. I prayed a bit in the car – and I've done that lots of times since.

I played rugby the next day and it was an absolutely fantastic day at Twickenham. To go down the tunnel and run out onto the Twickenham turf and to play rugby there was fantastic. But that day was nothing in comparison to the evening before. I then went through the rest of the Alpha course.

I think Nicky's prayer was the starting point for me. I haven't turned my life round completely – I'm still struggling in lots of areas. I know it may sound strange, but I've had my eyes opened to so much in such a short space of time and I know what life is about now. Silly things like walking in the street and speaking to people saying, 'Hello. How are you?' Whereas before I was so entrenched in my own problems.

I'm reading the Bible. I like to read a bit every day even if it's only a couple of pages. I'm working my way through it. I would never have read the Bible before. If someone had said to me a year before Alpha that I'd be reading a page of the Bible every day I would have said, 'OK, mate, there's a straitjacket for you.' The only thing I ever used the Bible for was to swear on in court – but it meant nothing when you think of the amount of times I told lies in court with the Bible. Now it's 'the' book.

I pray now as well. I started praying soon after I met Nicky. I started off praying sitting in church with my head in my hands or kneeling at home in the quietness when no one was around and just saying a few things. I'm developing. If someone had said to me two years ago, 'In two years you're going to be kneeling down quietly at home praying,' I would have said something like, 'Go and bang a tambourine, mate.' Now I think it's fantastic.

Until I came to Holy Trinity Brompton I really didn't know what life was about. Although I had a life I had no life really. But now it has shown me the way and the true way. I know I've got loads more to do where my relationship with God is concerned but at least I know which way I'm going, whereas before I didn't know which way I was going.

As well as working on my relationship with God, I've got to work on my relationship with Linda and my kids. With Linda things have taken a turn for the better. I'm happy at home. I'm getting an awful lot more out of my marriage now.

I was driving round the M25 the other day and I was playing this worship tape. I then had a vision of Jesus come into my head and I thought, 'I want to tell people that he's real.' People may say, 'Oh, it's not true,' but I want to say, 'It is true because I've seen him.'

Simon Pinchbeck continues to be a member of Holy Trinity Brompton, where he is involved in the church's prisons ministry.

3 THE RUGBY PLAYER
THE STORY OF UGO MONYE

Ugo Monye's professional rugby career rose meteorically when the Harlequins winger was selected for England and the British Lions. But it was not all such plain sailing. Here he tells his story.

My first love was football. Arsenal was just round the corner from where we lived and I followed it massively. I love Arsenal. When I was twelve, I went to Lord Wandsworth College, a boarding school in Hampshire. I was the first boy in our family to go away to boarding school but I was really happy about it. I knew I was going to a good school and would get a good education.

Before going there I'd never touched a rugby ball but suddenly I was given this squashed football and told to pick it up and run. At first my handling skills weren't good at all but when I caught the ball (which was infrequently) I could run with it. When he saw this, the coach must have thought, 'Well, if we can give him a bit more coaching then something might come of it . . .' And he stuck with me. I played in the first team at school for my final two years – on the wing.

Jonny Wilkinson and Peter Richards were also at the school, although several years ahead of me. Everyone in the school looked up to them because they were the guys who were playing England Under-21s. Jonny showed incredible determination from an early age. He'd be outside training – even after school. He spent his lunch hours kicking while we'd be chasing girls or playing football. That work ethic has put him where he is today.

I was quite fortunate because my school sports coach Tim Richardson was in contact with a guy called Colin Osborne in the Harlequins Academy. He said I wanted to play a bit of rugby and could I come down? So I went to a couple of training sessions.

Then I was given a jersey and asked to play a game. I was so excited. I polished my boots, ironed my kit and got everything prepared. I got on the train to Twickenham, walked up to the Stoop [Harlequins' ground], went into the changing room, opened my gym bag and realised I'd forgotten my boots. I couldn't believe it. I looked around at the other guys there. They looked like they'd been on steroids for the last five years. They were big guys. And there I was – about to play a rugby match in my school shoes.

I said to Colin, 'Mate, I've forgotten my boots.'

He said, 'It's all right. Go and speak to the kit man and see if he's got anything.' I went up to the kit man (whose nickname was Ratty) and said, 'Mate, have you got any size eleven boots?' He said, 'Yeah, I've got one Nike and one Reebok – that's all I've got.' So I had to take them. I played that first game in odd boots! But we won 51–0, which kind of made up for it a bit.

When I left school my mum really wanted me to go to university. My sister had gone off to law school and done really well. So it was a big deal when I said to Mum, 'I'm not going to uni, I'm going to play rugby.' I told her about this great club, Harlequins, and explained that I had a chance of playing for them. At first I went to Harlequins on a kind of a trial basis to prove to my mum that I could really make a go of this. Six games later I was offered a contract, so the gamble paid off. That was in 2001.

The contract I got was an apprenticeship contract for just one year. Within a few weeks I had trials at England Under-19s – but then I broke my foot. So that was me done. In hindsight it was probably the best thing that ever happened to me. I'd come out of school weighing twelve stone and was so small and weak that I would have been like a rag doll to some of my first teammates. I was very brittle and not hardened. I wasn't ready for premiership rugby. But breaking my foot gave me a whole season to be in the gym and the progress I made was invaluable. The next season I was back playing again and they offered me a new contract for two years because of all my hard work in the gym. I made my first team debut that year [2002] against Glasgow and have never looked back.

My first try for Harlequins was against Wasps, who had been on an unbeaten run of eighteen games. Quins were eighth or ninth in the table. We were playing away from home and everyone wrote us off. In the end I scored two tries and we won the game.

My second contract meant that I could afford to live away from home. I was desperate to get out and I moved to Teddington with a couple of other guys from the club.

Church was a massive culture in our family and we used to go to a vibrant Pentecostal church every Sunday. But when I moved away from home, I stopped going. Saturday nights became a big event, so Sunday mornings were spent in bed recovering or watching TV. The thought of going to church quickly became a distant memory – nice, but not something that I felt was important. My mates weren't going and I did what my friends did. If they were going out for breakfast on a Sunday morning then I wanted to be there.

I was attracted by the bright lights of London and I wanted to see it all. I felt, 'OK, this is my time now. Let's get out and see what's going on.' I'd never been nightclubbing and drinking in bars before. I felt as if I was a real adult and I wanted to do adult things. I wanted to be immature and a bit silly.

I stayed playing first team Harlequins and I also played England Sevens for three years from 2002. We travelled the world including Australia, Hong Kong, Singapore, Dubai, LA, New Zealand and South Africa. We played in some huge stadiums jam-packed with 50–60,000 people. As a nineteen-year-old it blew me away. It was crazy.

2002 was a funny year for me because at the start of the season I went to trials for England Under-21s and didn't make it. I was told I wasn't good enough. A week after that I got selected for the England Sevens team. We flew to Australia and won the tournament for England – the first time they'd ever won an IB7s tournament. It was ridiculous. I never expected to be there, let alone win it. After that I got promoted to England Under-21s, came back the very next weekend and played for England 21s against France.

I scored two tries on my debut. So it was a ridiculous two weeks of, first, not being in the England 21s, then travelling to Australia with the England Sevens, winning that, coming back and then playing for England 21s and doing well.

I played for England 21s for a second season and we won the Six Nations Grand Slam. We were the first team to win the Grand Slam. So it was another amazing year. Because my rugby was going well I was really happy. I had lots of friends, I was in the first team and I felt good about myself. But it was all me, me, me.

At the end of that season I got selected to go on tour with England, so that was brilliant. But things did change the next season – in 2005–06. Harlequins got relegated and I was really angry. I spoke to my mum and she said, 'It's all right. God's got a plan for you.' But I didn't understand that at all. I was angry and really upset. I thought if God loved me then why would he do this?

My career had been going exactly as I imagined it from school level – playing through the age groups, playing for Quins, going on tour with England . . . and then there was this massive dip, with Quins getting relegated.

I massively wanted to leave Quins. All I wanted to do was to keep playing premiership. But there were no clauses in my contract for me to leave. So I went to the CEO and said, 'I want to go' and he said, 'Not a chance.' I spoke to everyone I could, including my agent and other clubs (to get them to buy me out of my contract) but Harlequins were having none of it.

I look back now and relegation's not a good thing for anyone, but we needed that at Harlequins. We came back up within the year. We only lost the one game and we won the Powergen Cup, so it was a really successful year. The crowds at Harlequins were incredible. They were always there, still buying the merchandise, still coming to cheer us on at away trips – even though we played on some terrible pitches.

That was a year of growing up for me as a sportsman. When you're used to the luxuries of massive changing rooms and beautiful pitches and all the rest of it, then going to some parks where one man and his dog turn up and having to play your best and get yourself motivated and geed up week in, week out, for ten months of a season – it was really tough. But I look back at it now and I needed that because it really grounded me. It's made me a better professional and a better rugby player.

In 2006 we were back in Premiership rugby so I was happy. I felt as if I'd kind of paid my dues. I'd been off the radar for a season so I had to rebuild my career – and I was looking forward to that challenge. But in the end I was plagued with injuries. I had a lot of problems with my back, joints, knees and ankles. I played two or three weeks on and then I'd be out for four, then I'd come back for one and be out for two. My whole season was like that. There was no real stability. We started the season really well up until December. We were getting good reports from the England coaches. Then in December I broke my ankle. I was out for six weeks at a really critical time in the rugby season. January is when England's Six Nations squad is decided and I really felt I was in the running.

I was talking to Dean Richards, our coach, who was talking to the guys across the road at the RFU. And there were good reports coming back. But that got blown out of the water when I got injured. I came back six weeks later and within two weeks I'd broken my sternum and was out for another eight weeks. So to lose fourteen weeks out of a season is a massive chunk. After four weeks out, I worked my butt off during pre-season for 2007–08 and I felt that it had really paid off. We started the season playing London Irish at Twickenham. It was a massive game that we won and I played well.

Then I went into training the following Monday and was doing some sprint training, jogging at about 50 per cent, when I collapsed on the floor. My back just broke down. I was paralysed for about a week. I couldn't walk, stand up or go to the toilet by myself. I was in searing agony. I stayed at a friend's house for four days, just lying on the floor of his living room. I couldn't go to my house because I live on the first floor of an apartment and I couldn't get up the stairs.

I thought my season was over. Through all this, my mum was praying massively. Then, after four weeks, it all cleared up. It was a total mystery. No one knows what happened. I suppose that's when my attitudes changed a bit. It was then that I started thinking that something had really got to change. I'd described myself as a Christian for all these years but I hadn't really acted like one and I felt a really big hypocrite. I kept getting these questions in my mind: 'How can I be a better person?' At that point I was going to church with my mum and dad every couple of months maybe. Then one morning in October I was lying in bed and thinking about what more I could do. I went into training that day and I got chatting to a masseuse called Rachel.

I said, 'What are you up to this week?' She said, 'I've got a Bible study on Wednesday.' I was like, 'OK, that's cool . . . So you go to church then?'

'Yeah, I go to church.'

'What church do you go to?'

'HTB in Kensington.'

I hadn't heard of HTB but I asked, 'Have you heard about this Alpha?' Driving past churches on my way to training I'd seen lots of Alpha banners with, 'Is there more to life than this?' They had also advertised it in my parents' church in Windsor. She said, 'Yeah, I did it last term.'

I said, 'Tell me, what was it like?'

She went, 'It changed my life.'

For me that's a big statement to make, but knowing what a nice girl she was and how genuine she was, I knew she wasn't the type to make a statement like that loosely. I thought, 'Well, if you can make a statement like that then it's probably worth finding out a bit about it.' The next day she got me some information and said, 'Alpha's starting next week. Do you want to go on it?' I was like, 'Yeah.' With all these questions bugging me in my head, I knew I had to. So I went home and asked my flatmate, Damien who is French and comes from a Christian background, 'Mate, have you heard of Alpha? Do you fancy doing the Alpha course with me? I'm definitely doing it whether you do it or not.' I was really bullish about it, so he agreed to come. So the two of us turned up on Alpha at Holy Trinity Brompton in October 2008.

I was expecting it to be about twenty guys sat in a room. But when I went into the church I could not believe it. I was overwhelmed and had goose bumps as I was walking in. There were about five or six hundred people. There was beautiful food laid out, everyone was smiling and looked happy and I was welcomed into my group. There was a really good mix of ages – that's another thing that appealed to me, the fact that it's for everyone. Damien couldn't believe it either. We were both in the same group. Nicky Gumbel spoke that night about Jesus and his life. I was shocked by all the evidence – the facts, figures and dates.

After that first week I couldn't wait to go back to Alpha. I was so excited. The group was amazing – it was so nice. What struck me and Damien was the respect everyone had for each other, regardless of where you came from or what your beliefs were. You could voice your opinion and everyone would listen. There were no hidden agendas. It was just beautiful. There was a lot of love in the room. Sally led our group – she was amazing. Damien and I went back each week. In the meantime my matches were going great. We were winning. I wasn't getting injured and I was playing really well.

I couldn't go on the Alpha weekend because I play at weekends and so I missed out. Damien couldn't make it either as he was away in France. On week four I got invited to church on Sunday so we met as a group and went to the 5 p.m. service.

We absolutely loved it. It was brilliant. I'd enjoyed church when I was a kid, but this was the first time I'd been to church because I wanted to be there. It was off my own back and I liked that. I did the whole course and every week it just got better. By the end I'd gained such a desire to do more in the church and learn more. I think at the end of one week someone asked if we wanted to recommit to God or give our lives to God. So I sat there and prayed for all my sins to be forgiven, to have a fresh start and to commit myself to God. I wanted a new beginning, a new chance.

I don't really read books much, but around week five I started reading *The Purpose-Driven Life* by Rick Warren. It was an amazing book. I absolutely loved it. I also started reading a passage of *Daily Bread* every night and praying before going to bed.

I realised many things about prayer. Before, I thought prayer had to be almost a ceremonial thing, where you had to be on your knees. But now I realised that God's probably as approachable as my dad or my friends. So we chat about anything. It affected my attitude. I came out openly and told all my friends and teammates I was a Christian. It came out one night when Arsenal were playing on a Wednesday and my mates were like, 'Are you coming round to watch the football?' And I said, 'Well, no, I've got Alpha.' And they were like, 'Yeah, right! See you at 7.30.' But I wouldn't show up. So they all knew about it.

By Christmas Harlequins were starting to struggle a bit and had got on a bad run, not winning a game in about eight or nine games. This was in the Heineken Cup.

But I was playing well and Brian Ashton [the England manager] was on the phone to Dean saying, 'You know, we're looking at Ugo . . .' We had a player appraisal, where you sit down with the coaches and talk about the season, and they said, 'We're really pleased with you. Keep your head down – we think England are going to come calling.' I was chuffed to bits. I prayed about that. I suppose my main prayer was to be injury-free because I knew if I could get on the pitch and play consistently then I'd further my career. So I prayed for fitness.

It came to January and everyone was saying, 'Ugo, you're going to be in the England squad – it's great.' But I didn't want to talk about it too much, I just wanted to focus on the next game and the training.

Then the squads were announced. There are two squads – a main Six Nations squad and then there's England A squad. I wasn't in either of them. That was a big, big blow. I was absolutely gutted. There's a good few wingers in this country, a lot of talented guys, but I still felt as if I was playing better than a lot of them. Previously, I'd have got angry and I'd have blamed God – 'How could you do this to me?' – as if he owed me something. But this time I prayed and my attitude changed massively. I sensed that it was going to be all right in the end.

Since then it's been going really well. The Quins are flying and I couldn't be happier. I'm Quins' top try scorer at the moment and I've recently signed for another two years.

I prayed with my family before signing the contract and the message was loud and clear to stay at Harlequins.

After that first Alpha course I did a second one as a helper. I wanted to get involved more and I loved it. It gave me an opportunity to maybe help other guys like me. I had a great group. I saw people's lives change massively. I'm leading a group with Jamie Haith this time – my third course. The best thing is when people say, 'You've changed big time.'

I'm so much more settled now and I'm a happier person. I feel as if I have substance to my life now, which I never had before. The only things that I had in my life before were materialistic and temporary. I was never satisfied. But I am now.

In February 2008 I was playing Wasps at home. I'd spoken to my dad during the week and he'd said, 'You're a sportsman, Ugo, and you have an opportunity to spread the Word. There are other sports stars who go out and spread the gospel. What I want you to do is to write a message on your T-shirt, and if you score a try I want you to show it to the crowd.'

I was like, 'Dad, what are you doing to me?' But I agreed. The night before the game I wrote a message on my white T-shirt with a big marker pen: 'I love Jesus.' After I did it I was really relaxed about it. Then I got to the game and I was so pumped for the game I scored the best try I'd scored that season. I was about sixty yards out and I got the ball, beat about four players and scored in the corner. I got up, raised two hands in the air, walked over to the crowd and lifted up my top. And they went crazy. I'm not sure if they understood or if they thought I was getting naked like a Chippendale. But they started roaring. There were about fourteen thousand people in the crowd.

None of the players saw it because they were all behind me. On the Sunday a couple of guys went to England training and saw my try on video. On the Monday there were photos on the internet and the lads were like, 'Have you seen what Ugo did?' It was crazy – guys were asking me, 'Are you OK?' One text I was sent read, 'Have you killed someone? Are you looking for forgiveness?' It was ridiculous. Two weeks previously we'd started a rugby Bible study group with a couple of guys from Quins and a few guys from Wasps. The week after I did it the guys from Wasps said, 'Ah mate, awesome – well done for doing that.'

Since then, I've invited heaps of friends to Alpha. Last term four friends came along. One of them has had the biggest transformation I've ever seen. The way in which I view Jesus now is massively different. The grace and love that he's shown me have been amazing. I know he's looking after me.

Ugo Monye played for England in the Six Nations in 2009 and was selected for the British Lions tour of South Africa that year, scoring more tries than any other player. He continues to worship at Holy Trinity Brompton.

4 THE ACTOR
THE STORY OF JAMIE HINDE

Actor Jamie Hinde has starred in some of the West End's top productions – but at one point he found that the applause of 2,500 people left him numb. Here he tells his story.

My parents went through a pretty heavy divorce when I was about eleven. I was brought up by my mum and saw my dad once a week. Mum was a theatre director and at around the age of twelve I was in a show that she produced. It was *The Sound of Music* and I played Kurt. I loved the production and after that I started attending a local acting workshop on Saturdays. At the workshop I made some great friends. But at school it was a different story. I didn't fit in and went around with a group of 'left-outs' because we didn't play sport. I did very badly at school. I started off in the A stream and went down to the C stream. I hated it so much that I bunked off and in fact had more absences than anybody for a couple of years. I left at seventeen with hardly any qualifications and went to a drama college in Chiswick.

Then, when I was 18, an amazing thing happened. I got an audition for *The Wizard of Oz* with the Royal Shakespeare Company. It was an incredible contract – starting at Stratford-on-Avon, then moving to London – and I was offered the job. I had to make a difficult decision: my college was pleased for me but told me that if I took it, I would have to leave. I took the job. I played the part of Nikko, the flying monkey, and it was an amazing time. I had a flat in Stratford right on the River Avon. I got an Equity card from the RSC and was later invited to audition for their season.

I learned something from *The Tempest* for the audition, but when the time came I completely froze up. When I walked out of there, I was in tears, saying, 'I've absolutely blown it, big time.' The next day my agent phoned and I was just miserable. But she said, 'Jamie, haven't you done well?' I went, 'Why? What . . .?' And she said, 'I've just had a phone call from the RSC – they've offered you sixty weeks' work with the company – to play Balthasar in *Much Ado About Nothing* and Baldock in *Edward II*.'

I later asked the directors, 'Tell me how I got this job?' They said, 'You know when somebody walks in a room – it's not about drying up.' I then did two years with them – 120 weeks. We went between Stratford and London – and then to Newcastle, which was great. They offered me another year, doing a completely new season. But I took a big risk then and decided to come out. After that I was offered *The Madness of George III* at the National. I went to Alan Bennett's house to meet him and got the part of Papandick. After touring with that, I had a year out of work when everything dried up. It was a really weird time; nothing was clicking.

Then the RSC began casting a very big production – *Henry VI Part III* – in Stratford, which was going to tour all over the world. I went for it and got the juicy part of Clifford. Suddenly I had a year with the RSC flying to the Philippines, to South America, etc., on a very classy tour. That was an incredible year. I was twenty-five or twenty-six. We played in Los Angeles and I got a fantastic review in the *Los Angeles Times*. I was being invited to lavish parties and meeting very famous people. It was a really exciting time. When I was twenty-eight or twenty-nine I played Eric in *An Inspector Calls* in the West End – a really nice part. Towards the end of that job I said to myself, 'It would be quite nice to direct something now.' The next day I got a phone call asking if I'd go and teach at a drama college. So I went to teach there while I was in between acting jobs. By then I'd bought a lovely flat in Winchmore Hill, north London.

Then they asked me to direct their third year final play – which I did. I'd never experienced fulfilment like it. I felt very proud of it. A producer came to see the play and said he'd back it for a run in London. But it wasn't the right time as the students were in the middle of their final year. I then produced and directed a few productions with the company I set up called Fly Monkey.

But something inside me was dissatisfied and I went on a spiritual search. I read every spiritual book going – books by Deepak Chopra, books on Buddhism, Taoism. Then I decided to return to acting and auditioned for *The Lion King*, which was running at the Lyceum in London. That was in 2003. I did seven auditions for Ed, the stupid, clowning hyena. With him you do the holiday cover for Scar [the evil lion], Timon [the meerkat] and Zazu [the bird]. So I was auditioning for four parts, and I just went for it. One morning I was near to jacking it in. My voice was croaky and I was tired. But in the end I got the job.

It was very well paid (Disney look after you very well indeed) and physically very demanding. But being a performer didn't have the same buzz for me that it used to have. I couldn't feel it in the same way.

I remember one night I was playing Scar – one of the lead roles – in front of 2,500 people and I stood there and thought, 'I don't feel anything . . .' It was a really strange thing. Then, during the latter part of my year there, I attended the final three sessions of the Theatreland Alpha course, which was run between shows on a Wednesday. I had loads of questions. My big question was, 'I believe I'm a good guy. Why should you be allowed into heaven and not me? Why is it exclusive?'

Soon after that *The Lion King* made me a very lucrative offer to stay on. You earn so much money there that most people stay. But I decided to leave. I just felt there was something else. When I left I didn't know what I was going to do.

At the end of 2004 a friend who is a Christian took me to a morning service at Holy Trinity Brompton – she told me it was an Anglican church where she sometimes went. Within seconds of arriving there I burst into tears. I didn't know why. As I sat there crying, the Alpha course was mentioned and she encouraged me to do the course. I said yes. That was January 2005.

When I arrived at Alpha I was in a bad way. I was drifting, with no real zest for anything. It was like, 'Why am I here? Do I want to be an actor?' I felt numb.

When I first turned up for Alpha, I had this cynicism. I looked around and thought, 'Is that a sincere smile? Are you real or not? Is this one big self-help group?' Every cynical bone in my body was going, 'What am I doing here?' But I had started to enjoy Nicky Gumbel's talks – and had been struck by something he had said about sin.

Then something amazing happened – the day that changed my life: 29 January 2005. I was only about two weeks into the course when I went away for the weekend to Cardiff to visit my godson for the first time. By this stage on Alpha something in my heart had clicked. And on the train I took the *Why Jesus?* booklet with me to read. After reading the booklet I came to the prayer at the back and decided to say it.

It was 5.15 p.m., it was dark outside and I was all alone in the carriage. So I said the prayer out loud. It was something along the lines of, 'Dear Lord Jesus, please forgive me for my sins. Thank you for dying on the cross for me. I ask you to come into my life, heal my life and guide my life.' And I can't explain what happened, but it was the most amazing, profound experience. I expected nothing – I was just saying the prayer. But I said it with integrity, with force and with absolute meaning.

I was at peace, serene, joyful and blissful. I felt incredible. The Spirit was just coming into me and saying, 'Jamie, it's true. Let's go for it.' And I remember having an image of Jesus in me. I could see him – not looking at me, but it was like he was in me. It was a really overwhelming experience and it went on for about twenty minutes.

It says in *Why Jesus?* that you should tell somebody. So I told my Christian friend rather tentatively that night that I'd become a Christian.

The following week in our Alpha group I thought I wasn't going to say anything about what had happened to me – but I couldn't hold back. So I told them that I'd had this experience and had become a Christian. After that, everything changed for me. I'd be reading the Bible and it was like *The Matrix* – you open up a little thing and start delving into this new world.

At the Alpha weekend I had an overwhelming, unbelievable experience of the Holy Spirit. I was absolutely euphoric – high as a kite. I was beaming. We saw amazing things happen in our group. Most of them became Christians and we went on to become a home group. But it hasn't been easy. It has been a real process of taking a self-centred life and becoming God-centred. The practicalities of day-to-day surrendering are so hard. And the process has been going on ever since.

The following few months were the most incredible time. I've cried tears I didn't even know existed – tears that go right back to my parents' divorce. They were coming out from deep within. Since then I've helped on another Alpha course and have been reminded of what an incredible blessing it is to be a Christian. It's an amazing thing.

I know now that I want to serve God. I'm at that stage where I'm going, 'OK – use me . . .' I want to glorify God in every way I can. I feel very blessed.

Jamie Hinde is now married to Ruth. He has continued to act in many prominent productions in London and around the UK. They attend a church near their home in Brighton.

5 THE BIKER
THE STORY OF PETE DOBBS

Pete Dobbs, of Battersea, south London, enjoyed his reputation as a violent man. He took part in racist attacks, and was once hired to kill a man. Here he describes how a series of extraordinary events changed his life.

I've been to Chelsea Football Club all my life. My dad took me first, just the once, when I was about five and after that I used to go with a friend. It was all terraces then, no seats, and I used to stand in 'The Shed'. I didn't like school and used to hop the wag – bunk off – for weeks and weeks sometimes. I used to intercept the letters that they sent to my house so my mother never got them.

It was only after my dad died of a heart attack when I was fifteen that my mum explained to me that he had another home where he lived. He had a wife and would go home to her every night after I went to bed. When he died my mum and I went to where his wife lived to pay our condolences.

Soon after that I met Maureen, a girl my age, and I moved in with her and her family. My mum wasn't happy about it but I got on great with Maureen's parents. When I was seventeen we had a child, David, and we got our own place, a one-bed flat on the Mozart Estate in west London. It was quite a notorious estate full of bad people, drugs, guns – the usual stuff.

Soon I started getting into fights at the football. The head of Chelsea football violence then was a one-armed bloke called Babs who was known as the hard man of Chelsea. We'd fight against West Ham, Millwall, Cardiff – it didn't matter who it was. We'd meet up on a bit of waste-land or down a side street. Sometimes we'd go into a pub and smash it up – picking up chairs, ramming them through the windows, just causing trouble, until we got dispersed by the police.

I first got a motorbike when I was about fourteen and my first car at sixteen. I was pulled over a few times as a youth without a licence and insurance. I'd be given seven days to produce my documents but nothing happened when I failed to produce them. After leaving school I became an apprentice bricklayer for Southwark Council. It was a four-year apprenticeship but I did it in three years because my grades were good. I've always been good at that kind of stuff.

I started hanging about with the National Front when I was eighteen. I used to go on some marches. Sometimes a group of lads and I would go up Southall and abuse the foreigners – waving cricket bats, smacking a few about, picking on them randomly, beating them up. I became very aggressive. If a foreigner looked at me I might go over and say, 'Who the ****ing hell do you think you're looking at?' and start pounding into him. Sometimes they'd get badly hurt. I don't think I've ever killed anybody, but I've certainly steamed in a few times, kicking them in the head and stuff like that.

I started to go everywhere with the football. I've been hurt a few times, kicked to pieces, stamped on, punched. Once they whacked me in the kneecap with a baseball bat and I was in a wheelchair for six weeks. Once, when I was on my bike, a guy cut me up along the Blackwall Tunnel. There's a slip road to Hackney, with a concrete wall between the slip road and the main road. After he cut me up I parked on the hard shoulder, got off my bike, then walked round the concrete bollard to where he was stuck in traffic. I put my fist straight through his window. I punched him several times in the face and took his car keys, then jumped back on my bike and rode off with his keys and left him there.

During the day I'd be working as a bricklayer and in the evenings I wasn't very nice to Maureen. I'd never shout at her, row with her or raise my hand to her – I've never done that to a woman in my life – but I just had so much aggression, so much anger. I don't know why. I stayed with Maureen until I was twenty, but I couldn't give her the love she deserved, so I started not coming home. By then we had two sons – David and Peter. I disappeared from their lives when they were still very young. Basically I deserted them. Later she married someone else and I got a letter asking if

I'd mind her husband adopting the children. I signed the papers, thinking, 'Well, let them have a more controlled life . . .'

I ventured back down to New Cross and got to know a particular family there. One of the blokes in this family was a couple of years older than me and he used to do burglaries and stuff like that. I went on a couple of burglaries with him until one of his friends got caught for something and grassed us up. We went to prison for nine months. I spent my twenty-first birthday in jail, but it didn't bother me.

After I came out I got back into work – and worked hard. I was money motivated. I was a very good bricklayer, I was good at my trade and I brought in the money. In the eighties there was a lot of money in building, and we'd have a fairly new car every three years, two holidays a year – one abroad, one at home. But I still went to my footie, I couldn't pack that up. I still had a lot of rage and anger. I was so very bitter. Someone would only have to say something and I'd roar and bark at them, big time. People were frightened of me.

I met a girl called Karen and we had two boys – Lee and Don. Because I'd already lost my first two I didn't want to lose these ones. She wanted to get married but I said, 'No, take it or leave it.' I took my sons to football but they just weren't into it. Then my son became a Man U supporter and I said, 'No, no, no, I'm not having it – you ain't coming no more!' It wasn't a laughing matter – I was horrified.

The 'Chelsea Headhunters' appeared in the 1980s. That was my roughest period. Around that time I was approached by a family to pay me some money to do somebody. The family was a very well-known bad family in south-east London and they knew about me. They knew that if I was going to do something I would do it; I would never back down. So they offered me an amount of money and I agreed to do it. I had the photograph and went to the pub where this guy was supposed to be drinking, with a sawn-off shotgun under my coat. I sat there and had a couple of shandies while I waited for him to come in, but he never came. If he'd come I would've done him. I had no thought about it at all. I would have waited until he'd gone out of the pub, then I would've followed him out and done him. Bang. But he didn't come so I returned the weapon to the family and we rearranged it for another month down the line. Then two members of this family got caught for something else and got long-term imprisonments at Belmarsh.

I wasn't really in that gangster world. I got my feet wet, but I wasn't really in it. I got involved with buying and selling hash through the family and used to go round to their house and have a smoke, but that was about it. After about eleven years with Karen I went up to Manchester to work there. I would see Karen every weekend. There were six of us living in a big house in Manchester for two years, while we were building several projects.

Soon after I came back, Karen and I split up after she did the dirty on me. A mate phoned me at work to tell me she'd been sleeping with this Irish bloke. So I went round to the bloke's flat and smashed the door in. He was asleep and I dragged him out of bed and punched him until he was unconscious. Then I got a hammer and some six-inch nails out of my bag and I nailed his hands and feet to the floor. He woke up screaming. I told him, 'If you don't leave now, you'll be dead.' He went back to Ireland and never came back.

My elder brother David had come out of the army after about nine years. He had been in Ireland and got shot by the IRA so he had to come home. Then he had a brain haemorrhage and died. He was thirty-seven. I was devastated.

In about 1998, I met Mandy in the Asda car park. Her car had broken down and she asked me if I'd give her a jump-start. So I started her car up and offered to help fix it. Then she gave me her phone number and I rang her up and went round. It was like love at first sight for me. It was the first time I can honestly say I felt love for a woman – proper love. After about four weeks I moved in with her. During the day I was still very loud and had a lot of anger and rage – but the minute I got home I was like a different man with her. She fell pregnant and we had a little girl called Breeze. We also moved to Colchester and I started to forget my football days.

A couple of years later I proposed to her and she said yes. We got married on 1 May 2004. It was a civil wedding because she was divorced, so we couldn't get married in a church. Things were very happy.

Mandy had been a Christian before and she started going to the Salvation Army in Colchester. One Sunday every month the Salvation Army would have a feast, where anyone could come along and eat. So I used to go along, as I always loved my food. I only went for the food. I got to know the minister, John O'Driscoll, and he tried to persuade me to come along to a service. At first I always refused but then I started to go to the Sunday service at 10.30 a.m. They'd have all these songs and I started joining in. My favourite song is 'Amazing Grace' (because of the football terraces) so I soon got in with the flow of things. But I still thought nothing of it.

Then one Sunday in March 2007 I was sitting listening to John's sermon and all of a sudden I had these emotions. I could feel all this stirring inside my body. I didn't know what it was and I didn't like it. Then all of a sudden it was as if somebody had literally put their hand inside my stomach, grabbed me round my spine and just pulled me up. I got up and went to the front of the building where they have a place called a 'mercy seat' where you can kneel. I'd never knelt before. I knelt down and floods of tears started coming out. Then one of the Sally Army elders came over and started praying for me. All of a sudden I said, 'Look, I've been such a bad man. I don't know why but I've been so bad.' And I shouted it out in front of everybody – the whole church service stopped.

The elder who was praying for me said, 'Give it to the Lord . . . he'll forgive you.'

I said, 'I can't be forgiven for some of the things I've done.'

At that point I stood up because I wanted to get out of the church. But as I stood it was as if Mike Tyson had hit me with a right hook – I went down like a sack of spuds.

After about five minutes I got up. I was still in floods of tears. I couldn't stop crying and I felt so bad in myself as a human being. I got some cuddles and a bit of reassurance off the wife, but I couldn't cope with that. I went home. For the first time in my life I felt sorry – I don't think I'd ever said sorry to anybody. For the first time I felt pain, sadness, happiness – emotions I never knew I had. And the whole congregation – about fifty of them – was watching all this. When Mandy and I got home I was in bits so she rang up this soldier from the Salvation Army and said, 'Look, Pete's really in a bad way and I don't know what to do.' So I went over to him and he prayed over me.

He said, 'Pete, you've been touched by the Spirit.'

I said, 'Why would he want to touch me? What have I ever done?'

And he said, 'Pete, just let it out . . . He has forgiven you.' I started babbling to him and crying on his shoulder. It was amazing.

That evening when I watched Crimewatch, I saw how people had done bad things to other people and it had me in floods of tears again. I didn't go to work for nearly a week because I was so confused. Unknown to me, my wife Mandy had already decided she'd had enough of me. I'd never paid her enough attention. So we split up. The Salvation Army were praying for our marriage but she was having none of it. She asked for a divorce shortly afterwards. That was really weird when I thought I was changing so much.

I was working in London at the time so John, the minister, said to me, 'Go and see Major Alan Norton in London' (he's some top guy in the Salvation Army). So I went to him, told my story, begged for forgiveness from the

Lord, and on 5 June 2007 – Pentecost – he helped me to pray a prayer asking Jesus into my life. On that day my anger – including my road rage – and stress levels just went. I stopped smoking hash immediately. I used to smoke every evening. After that, he said, 'Pete, what do you want to do with your life?' I said, 'I want to do as much as I can for my Lord. If I can give, I'll give. If I can do, I will do. The old Pete Dobbs is dead. I'm a new guy now and I want to live my life right.'

He said, 'Pete, go to the Alpha course.'

I didn't have a clue what Alpha was going to do for me. He said that on Alpha I could grow and find out what God wanted for my life. He directed me to this church called Holy Trinity Brompton and I went along. But they were just finishing their summer course and I only got there for the last week. I looked around and I was amazed to see so many nice people in one place. I thought, 'I really want this.' I was itching to get onto the course. The next course started in September 2007.

I started going to a Salvation Army men's group on Mondays. On Tuesdays I was going to prayer evenings and I couldn't get enough of it. Then that September I started going to Alpha on Wednesdays. After Nicky Gumbel's talk that first week, I was like, 'Wow, this is amazing. I really love this,' for week after week. I was on a constant buzz.

I missed three football games because of Alpha. In the old days I would never have missed a Chelsea match like that – never in a million years. Football had always been first in my life. Then I went on the Alpha weekend in Chichester. That was awesome. I was like a junkie – a junkie for the Lord! I didn't know what to expect from the weekend but you could feel an electrical charge in the atmosphere. I was praying all weekend.

All my old friends say, 'Pete, you're a different person.' They can see the difference in me, big time. I don't sit there staring at people with a look of aggression on my face. I don't rant, I don't rave, I don't shout at them. I still cheer in football games but I don't sing the bad songs any more.

My language has changed – it used to be, 'F this, F that . . .' – especially in my work as a bricklayer foreman. But I don't swear any more and I don't abuse. If the guys who work for me slack I will have to sack them, but I won't need to abuse them.

I go to Tollington Park Church on Sunday mornings now and in the afternoon I go to Wandsworth Salvation Army.

I took a Tottenham fan to Chelsea recently. I would never have done that before. While we were at the match, I must have had six phone calls from friends saying, 'Pete, I've just spotted you coming into Chelsea, what you doing?' And I'd say, 'I'm with my friend, my Tottenham, Christian brother.'

'Oh you wuss!' and they'd rib me up a bit. But I can take it. They all know I'm a Christian and they think it's awesome. They're impressed. Now I get non-Christian friends – sometimes violent people, sometimes old drug-dealers – ringing me up and saying, 'Pete, would you say a prayer for such and such . . .?'

Apparently the definition of a psychopath is somebody who has no remorse for what they do. And people called me a psychopath. I didn't have any remorse for any of the things I did. I could have killed someone . . . I know that I have definitely been angry enough to do that. Whether it was the Lord stopping me from going that step further, I will never know.

Now I'm never alone. Jesus is there with me all the time. Sometimes on my way to work I talk to him on my bike – it could be any time. I feel so contented and so at peace. I've virtually lost everything that meant anything to me and yet I'm still smiling.

Some time after becoming a Christian I decided to look for my oldest sons – David and Peter – who I hadn't seen since they were small children. I went onto 'Friends Reunited' and looked up their mum, Maureen, and emailed her. We met up a couple of months later and she said, 'You're a changed man . . . You seem to be really mellow now.' Then David got in touch with me and after a few emails we decided to meet up. We first met in a pub at Earl's Court and I said my sorries to him. Meeting him again was really awesome.

Not long ago a car ran over my motorbike. I was visiting my boys, Lee and Don, and I heard crunch, crunch, crunch – some car had run over my motorbike. So I went up to the car and this little bloke got out. He was shaking. Before becoming a Christian I would have dragged him out of the car and battered him. This time I said, 'Are you all right, mate? Look, sit down, don't worry about it.'

He went, 'It's your bike . . .'

I said, 'Just sit there and chill, relax, catch your breath, make sure you're feeling fine. It's just a bike, don't worry about it.' Then my ex-partner, Karen, came out and asked, 'What's the matter?' And I said, 'He's run over my bike.' And she said, 'I never heard nothing.'

I said, 'Well, you wouldn't, you were indoors.'

She went, 'No, I didn't hear you shouting. I didn't hear you. Someone's run over your bike and you've not said nothing . . .!'

I said, 'Well, it's only a bike – what's a bike?'

So my life's turned full circle and I'm loving every minute of it. It feels like I'm a millionaire, it really does. I'd never read a Bible before becoming a Christian. Now I read a bit every day. Finding the Lord is the best thing that ever happened to me.

Now I can sense love. Before I couldn't give it or receive it. Now there's floods of it. I'm in awe of it all – I can't believe how lucky I am.

Since being a Christian, Pete Dobbs has done volunteer work with the Salvation Army and Alpha for Prisons. He has also been to Africa, where he and a group of other volunteers helped to build a school. He now lives in the north of England. He says, 'I thank God for knocking on my door and making me new.'

6 THE EXPEDITION MEMBER
THE STORY OF NIGEL THOMPSON

Nigel Thompson crossed the Atlantic with his friend TV adventurer Bear Grylls in an open boat back in 2003 in a voyage described in Bear's book Facing the Frozen Ocean. *Here Nigel tells his story.*

I was born in Newcastle-upon-Tyne. My father was in banking and my brother and I were sent to board at Durham School. We had this beautiful chapel at school but I saw the services as something to be endured rather than enjoyed.

I was big into sport. Rowing was my number one interest all the way through school and I was captain of the Boat Club. After school, I went to Oxford Brookes University and carried on rowing. Their rowing squad was very strong – third or fourth best university in the country. I sat at number three in an eight, in what's known as the powerhouse.

We trained hard. We'd get up at 6.00 a.m. and go off in a minibus to Wallingford, a twenty-minute drive from Oxford. We'd be on the river by 7.30 a.m. and would row for about two hours, then take a break, and then do another couple of hours. At weekends, we'd spend almost all day Saturday and Sunday on the river. Rowing is not like rugby or football where you can just turn up and put some jumpers on the ground for goalposts. A boat costs a lot of money and you can't do it part-time.

I had a very active social life at university. I remember my lecturer in the first year saying you can only do two things at university, but there were three options: socialising, work and sport. I chose a bit too much sport and social life! I'd say 90 per cent of my good friends today are from university.

I graduated from university in 1996 with a degree in Real Estate Management and immediately joined a surveying company in London. All I wanted to do was to go to London and see what it was all about. I had a lot of friends who'd grown up in London but I didn't know the place at all, so I was really excited about getting stuck into it.

I tried to carry on rowing but the conflict with my career was evident. Soon after I arrived in London I went along to Thames Rowing Club and on the first day, the guy in charge of the senior squad said: 'The kind of commitment we need is Monday, Tuesday and Wednesday mornings, Thursday and Friday evenings, two outings on Saturday and Sunday, and a couple in your own time.' I was starting out, building my career, and just thought it wasn't for me. I tried it for six months but gave up.

I worked for a big international surveying company called Healey & Baker and they were exciting times. My offices were in Hanover Square, in the heart of Mayfair, so right in the middle of everything. I worked on retail property, so there were lots of shopping centre developments. It was all about turning up early and leaving late. But I also had a really full social life in the first few years in London. Everyone wants to go out and have fun all the time.

After two years, I changed jobs and moved to Lunson Mitchenall. It was a small company of around fifteen people back then. It's now considerably bigger. We worked on the Lakeside shopping centre in Essex; Braehead Shopping Centre in Glasgow; the MetroCentre in Newcastle; and we also did a lot of city centre redevelopment.

I first met Bear through his wife Shara, who was a great friend of mine at university. We had a lot of mutual friends. I lived with Shara and her sister Annabel soon after we moved to London and Bear lived just round the corner so we'd spend a lot of time together.

Bear never really had a conventional job and I think he was a bit bemused by what I did in the office every day. He used to ring me up and say, 'I'm going to swim across the Thames this afternoon. Do you want to come?' This would happen on a Tuesday afternoon and I'd say, 'Well, I'd love to but I'm about to go into a meeting with some clients.' But we used to do a lot of madcap things together. We both loved boats and we each had very old, knackered speedboats that we used to bomb around the Solent in together. They were utterly unreliable and unsafe. He used to take Nima the dog and Shara. I'm not sure Shara enjoyed it as much as we did. Bear never really paid much attention to rules and regulations. He hasn't changed much.

I'm not sure Bear had done many big expeditions before Everest. It was a sponsored climb and I think there was a space available and he thought he'd go along. Some time after that Bear jet-skied around the UK for the RNLI with a few friends. I didn't get involved in any of that, but then Bear suggested we went around the UK in an RIB (an inflatable boat made of rubber – a sort of Land Rover of the seas). You can put an enormous engine on an RIB and they'll go through any kind of sea and won't tip over.

My first RIB had a 115-horsepower engine, meaning I could go at about 40–50 miles per hour, which is pretty fast on water. You can jump around in big seas and it's really good fun, and you can water ski. We loved it. Bear and I were both really interested in boats. So we thought we'd get one built and go around the UK and get sponsorship.

But then we read about a team that had tried to cross the Atlantic in an RIB but had failed, and were trying again. So we thought we'd give that a go. It sounded more fun than going around the UK.

This was in 2002. To start with it was just the two of us and Mick Crosthwaite, a very good friend of Bear's from school, who had also been on the Everest expedition. Then we needed someone who knew a lot about boats, so we asked a guy called Lt Andy Leivers, who was an engineer in the Royal Navy on HMS Newcastle, to join. He was really good to have on board because he had spent more time at sea than all of us put together.

Then we had to try and get sponsorship, which was all very amateur in those days. Bear would email me something and I'd try and print it out at work when no one was looking. I didn't initially tell anyone at work what I was doing. We tried to get a picture of an iceberg on the front of our proposal, because we were going via Greenland. You have to stop in Greenland and Iceland to refuel. You can't take the shortest, most direct route – which would be straight across from Newfoundland – because the boat can't carry enough fuel.

The only way to go is northwards up the Canadian coastline to the Nova Scotia coastline, then across to Greenland, then Iceland, and you finish in Scotland, on the north coast. The longest bit was probably from Greenland to Iceland, or Canada to Greenland – both bits were quite long.

We didn't realise how dangerous it was. We took a very broad-brush approach and probably didn't pay enough attention to detail, which is kind of how we did these things. There were all manner of boating specialists who wanted to offer their advice, and if I had a pound for every time someone said to me, 'You must be mad,' I'd be a very rich man.

We managed to get sponsorship for the boat and engine. Our biggest sponsor was a watch company called Arnold & Son, who are very high-end. None of us had heard of them and we wouldn't have expected them to sponsor us. The boat would have cost about £75,000, but it didn't cost us anything like that much because everyone was doing it at cost. It was twelve metres by three-and-a-half metres. My original RIB was five metres, so this was much bigger. Twelve metres sounds a lot but there wasn't much space for five people.

We also took a cameraman called Charlie Laing, who wasn't really a seafaring chap at all. I think he wondered what on earth he was doing.

We set off in August 2003. You can only really do it in August to ensure there isn't too much ice. We started off in Halifax, Nova Scotia. The boat was shipped over by container, which a company very kindly sponsored us for. I took three weeks off work. My company was actually one of our sponsors and my colleagues were very excited. They were a great bunch of guys and everyone was interested in what we were doing.

Our main worry was being wet and cold for a long time in rough seas. We were also worried about breaking down. The seas could be horrendous, so if you broke down and had little control of the boat, you could be in a lot of trouble. It would be hard to get the engine going again, and when you lose power, the boat turns broadside to waves and that's when you're in the danger zone.

The biggest fear was that in big seas, the boat could capsize in the middle of the night 400 miles away from any kind of land, with icebergs all around you. You'd survive just minutes. We did have a life raft on the boat, but in the event of anything going wrong, the thought of just calmly swimming towards the boat, climbing into the life raft, setting off your satellite beacon and waiting to be rescued, is just ridiculous. It's just not going to happen.

I'd never seen an iceberg before and there are a lot of them around, even in August. Some float just beneath the surface, so if you are going at speed at night and they don't show up on any radar, then the boat could go over. At night, it's best to turn off all the lights in the boat and the instrument lighting and just see by the moon and stars.

We'd usually have one person driving, one person navigating and three would be sleeping, eating and resting. But we didn't get much sleep. Waves would be coming over and showering you, pulverizing you. There was water in the boat all the time. We'd wear these helmets, with a visor like the ones the lifeboat guys wear. They'd protect you if you were thrown around in the boat because there was a lot of sharp metal on the floor, and sharp edges. The last thing you want is for your head to hit bare metal. And we wore these dry suits, with rubber seals around the neck and the arms, which are supposed to keep you dry. But water is always going to get in. When you've got a wall of freezing salt water hitting you at speed, hour after hour, nothing is going to keep the water out. It came in around the neck and our heads were exposed. The helmet kept the worst out, but you were still open to the elements to a certain extent.

The worst bit of weather we encountered was between Greenland and Iceland. It was beautiful leaving Greenland. As the sun set we thought, 'This is brilliant, this is what it's all about.' We'd spoken to a weather station at the edge of Greenland via radio, and they had said, 'As long as you don't hang around you should be OK.' So we thought, 'That's fine then, let's go.'

Then about ten to fifteen hours into the journey it started to get choppier, but we carried on. I was monitoring the barometer, which is the best indication of a low-pressure system, and it was dropping like a stone. I thought there must be something wrong with it. There was a barometer on my watch too and I thought that had gone wrong. Every hour or so the pressure dropped a couple of millibars. The graph was a vertical drop. It was getting dark and I was thinking, 'This really wasn't part of the plan.'

That night it got windier and windier. A few waves started coming over the front, and as it got darker it got worse. I was looking at the watch and it was still dropping, and I was thinking we were potentially in a lot of trouble. We weren't in the business of turning around, so we carried on into the night and it just got worse. Eventually every single wave was washing over the boat. In those conditions you're only doing ten to twelve knots, which is frustratingly slow. In perfect conditions, the boat can probably do twenty to twenty-five knots.

The gale went on all night; I think it was a force nine or ten or something. It was really uncomfortable and unpleasant. There are no photos of the bad times because it was night and everyone was hanging on for dear life. I took the view that I didn't want to be strapped into the boat if it went over, which was a real danger. I'd rather be free to swim about and then work out what to do.

We didn't have a doctor on board and we had very limited medical training. We had a first aid kit and that was about it. I have nightmares thinking about what could have happened if someone really had injured themselves.

That night, we also lost all the electrics on the boat, so we were navigating with a handheld backup GPS, which wasn't ideal. The radar also went down, and the beacon we had that would transmit our location every couple of hours to people back home so they could see where we were – well, that also went down in the middle of the night.

Throughout the expedition, we had great assistance from another naval contact, Captain Pennefather. He had been coordinating the land side for us and by this point was very, very close to sending out a search and rescue party from Greenland, which would have been awful.

Everyone at home, including our families, was assuming the worst. We just disappeared off their monitors in the middle of the night. When we arrived in Iceland we made contact with the team via mobile phone and they said, 'We haven't heard from you in eighteen hours. We thought the worst.' We stayed one night in Iceland, long enough to repair the boat before continuing on our way. A guy who was organising the fuel for us put us up in his house. We slept in sleeping bags on the floor.

The whole trip took seventeen days. We were completely shattered when we arrived in Scotland. We hadn't slept for more than twenty or forty minutes at a time, apart from in Iceland where we got about five or six hours. At the end of it all, I suppose it was a bit of an anticlimax. We'd been planning it for two years and the moment it was over I had to go back to work.

So we did it. We were the first people to cross the Atlantic Ocean unassisted in an open RIB.

Just a few days after we finished, I was brought back to reality with a bump. I had a meeting with clients in Nottingham and I turned up thinking it was all a bit surreal, talking about shopping centres in Nottingham after what I'd just been through.

I always knew Bear was a Christian but he didn't ever force anything on me and we rarely talked about it. It was of no interest to me whatsoever. I assumed it was part of him being a bit eccentric, unconventional. I don't think Shara was a Christian when we were at university. She certainly never talked about it. About six of my friends – including Bear and Shara – did Alpha when we first moved to London. I couldn't understand why they were doing it. Bear invited me and Mick Crosthwaite to an Alpha supper some time before our RIB trip across the Atlantic. I had never set foot inside Holy Trinity Brompton and didn't know who Nicky Gumbel was at all, but something he said that night resonated with me. Nicky was talking about how many of us are just existing and waiting for the next thing, like 'when I'm promoted', or 'when I get paid next month'. That really resonated with me. At that time I was thinking, 'When I get paid next month everything will be fine,' then 'When I get my year-end bonus everything will be fine,' then 'When I buy a new house I'll be happier.' I've never forgotten that talk.

But I did nothing about it. Mick and I left the supper in perhaps a cynical frame of mind, thinking it was all a bit weird but the supper was nice. And that was it for six years or so.

I got to know Nicky a bit through Bear. They played squash together and I'd go to the gym with Bear a lot when I was training for the boat trip – so I saw Nicky then. But I never expressed any interest in church at all and Alpha rarely came up in conversation. Then last September Bear was being interviewed by Nicky at HTB and invited me along. He suggested we have supper afterwards, so I went with Shara and her mother.

Nicky announced that the new Alpha course would be starting in a few days and I remember whispering to Shara that I was thinking about doing it.

She said, 'Yeah, you should,' and I said, 'Well, maybe, I don't know.'

Afterwards, we went for supper in the vicarage. Pippa – Nicky's wife – was serving up soup and Shara suddenly said, in front of Pippa, 'Nigel's thinking of doing the Alpha course.'

I said, 'Well, I didn't quite say that . . .' But Pippa said, 'Oh, that would be wonderful. You could be in our group.'

Then Bear overheard and said to Nicky that I was thinking of doing the Alpha course, and Nicky said, 'That's wonderful, Nigel, why don't you join our group?' So one throwaway comment to Shara half an hour before had now got me totally involved. I said 'Yes, that would be lovely,' but inside I was thinking, 'How am I going to get out of this?'

A week later, I was at work and thinking what on earth had I got myself into. Bear texted me asking me if I was going to go. I said 'Yes, probably,' thinking I'd be letting him down if I didn't. So I went. I drove into the car park and sat there with the lights off so no one could see me. There seemed to be thousands of people and I was looking around thinking, 'Is there anyone normal here, anyone I could be friends with?' At that very moment I got a text from Bear saying, 'Are you there yet?'

So I went in and registered and then Pippa grabbed me and said 'It's great to see you, we're so pleased you came, come and join our group . . .' It was a fantastic group, all quite similar in age – just really cool people. From that first week I genuinely thought it was interesting. There were things I hadn't given any thought to – like who'd written the Bible, or when it was written. I probably didn't realise it was a compilation of hundreds of people's contributions over hundreds of years. I barely knew the difference between the Old and the New Testament. That wasn't really part of religious education at school.

I'd also known the artist Charlie Mackesy for about ten years through Bear, so it was interesting hearing him give the first talk. I didn't know anything about that side of his life. He spoke very well. The weeks went on and Alpha became the highlight of my week. People kept asking me to things on Wednesdays and I said I couldn't go because I was doing this Alpha course. They asked why and I said, 'I'm not really sure why, but I'll let you know.' I couldn't make the first weekend away – when the rest of my group went – so I had to go on the second weekend. Not only was I on a weekend with the potential of feeling totally out of my comfort zone, but I was also with people I didn't really know.

I remember driving down there; I was giving a few girls a lift. And I was thinking to myself, 'I must have better things to do on a Friday night.' I hadn't told any of my close friends what I was doing because they'd think I'd gone mad.

The church curate Jamie Haith was leading the weekend and I joined Jamie and Andy's group, which was fantastic. He made me feel utterly at ease, he's such a warm, humorous guy. Jamie led the Holy Spirit session on Saturday evening and afterwards he came over and asked if I'd like him to pray for me. Well, nobody had ever asked to pray with me before, so I thought, I can't really say no. So I said yes. It felt amazing.

And then he asked if I'd pray for him. And I'm thinking, 'Right, what do I say now?' So I thought, 'Say whatever comes in your mind, just thank God for everything. If my friends could see me now they'd think I'd gone completely potty.'

I felt like this was so far out of my comfort zone it wasn't even in sight. This was on a whole new level to the frozen ocean. I'd rather have run across the frozen ocean than pray for somebody, especially someone in Jamie's position.

There was no thunderbolt for me on Saturday evening. That came more on the Sunday morning when Paul Cowley, Head of Social Transformation for HTB, did a talk about how our faith affects the way we live our lives. It was when I was driving home on Sunday evening that I first genuinely felt different. I thought yes, perhaps there is a different way to live my life. Why don't I give it a go? What have I got to lose?

I thought, 'Why don't you just try and be a better person, starting now?' I thought I'd just try and if it didn't work out, well, the Alpha course finishes in a few weeks and that's that.

I used to pray before the Alpha course in a very amateur way. Then, before bed, I'd just thank somebody – well, I called him God. Even then I didn't really believe in God but, you know, you think what's the harm in it? After the weekend, my prayers were more like, 'Try to make me a better person and make me treat others better.'

At the next Alpha evening, it became clear that everyone had had very different experiences. Some were breaking down in tears and others were thinking, 'What a waste of a weekend.' I was probably somewhere in the middle.

Wednesday nights had become a major pillar of my life by then. By the end of Alpha, I definitely felt very different about my life. At the time I was in the process of handing in my notice at work to start up a new business venture. I would usually worry about that but I felt quite calm about it. I knew there'd be a few hiccups along the way but I just felt calm. I started planning this new business around the first week of Alpha. It worries me a bit. I'm giving up a career I've been working at for twelve years to go into the wilderness. It's a similar kind of property-based business, which I'm starting with a New Zealander friend of mine. I've been very keen to escape my current job and start something on my own. Succeeding or failing is secondary, I've just got to give it a go. I genuinely do feel that God is with me and behind me every step of the way. If the business succeeds, then great. But if it fails, then I'll do something else.

I do feel like there's somebody looking after me. I feel that someone has a sort of plan for me and knows what I'm going through and is there beside me. It is like having an invisible friend.

Now I'm obsessed with going to church. If you'd have said this would happen six months ago I'd have thought you were mad.

I was away at a birthday party in the Cotswolds recently. We all went out to lunch on Sunday and then it got to about four o'clock, we were all sitting in the pub garden, and I said, 'I've got to go'. I'm sure my friends all think I'm utterly bonkers. They know I'd done this ten-week course but they thought that would be the end of it and then I'd be back. But no, it just gets more and more. Actually having a relationship with Jesus is something I find difficult to grasp and recognise.

I'd call myself a Christian now, though I don't know when I became a Christian. I go to church. I try and lead a different life from six months ago. I have different morals from before, I think. I hope I treat people better. I'm definitely happier; I don't worry as much.

I'm doing the One Year Bible, so I get the email every morning, try to read the relevant passage and then read Nicky's comments, which I find very helpful. I read it at work or whenever I get a moment really – or I read it on my BlackBerry sometimes. I pray most days although my prayers aren't very long or sophisticated.

I think Bear thinks it's wonderful that I'm going to church. I bump into Charlie [Mackesy] quite a lot at the six o'clock service. He told me he said to Bear, 'What have you done? What's happened to Nige?' and Bear said, 'I don't know, I'm not sure what's happened to him, but something's worked.'

Nigel Thompson now lives in Hampshire where he attends a local church with his wife and family.

7 THE THIEF
THE STORY OF DAVE TAYLOR

Dave Taylor spent his early years in and out of jail. A drug addict and habitual thief, he could see no way out of his downward spiral. Then God began to touch his life and he went on an Alpha course in Brixton prison.

When I was born, my mother and father were running a fish and chip shop. When I was five my mum caught my father having an affair with a young girl who used to babysit me and my older brother. I haven't had any contact with my real father since then. My mum, my older brother and I got into a taxi and went straight round to my grandparents' house. They lived in east London, right next to the West Ham ground. We lived there for a bit and I started to go to junior school there. My mum met my stepfather Fred while working as a barmaid in a club. Eventually my nan, who worked with the local council at the time, managed to get a council property for us, so we all moved in together – Mum, Fred, my brother and me. I was somewhere between five and seven then. Some time after that we all moved to Essex.

Our family was far from happy. There was a lot of domestic violence. My stepfather used to beat my mum up quite regularly. He left my mum to pay the bills and she was useless. Instead, she'd go out and buy comfort food and clothes. So when the debt collectors and bailiffs turned up, my stepfather would say, 'Why haven't you paid the bills?' to my mum. Then there'd be an argument and before you knew it she'd be beaten up again. It was very hard. I can remember Mum being knocked to the ground and out cold quite a few times.

As I got older, I tried to stop him and that's when he'd lose his temper and have a go at me. He never hit me full in the face but he's a big guy, twenty-odd stone. When you've got a big guy like that on top of you, it's very frightening. From an early age my brother tried to get away because he couldn't handle it. He went to join the Navy, leaving me and my half-sister Joanna.

But I still liked my stepfather. He brought me up and always had a lot of time for me. We went on holidays together and went out as a family at weekends – to the cricket and stuff like that.

I can remember smoking cigarettes at thirteen. Then within a couple of months it was marijuana with some of the people I knew in the area. Then it was glue-sniffing and then it was nicking the Scotch and the vodka from the house and sneaking away. My friends introduced me to all this stuff, which normal teens do, but I don't know if it's me having an addictive personality or what. I isolated myself from really early on and it was basically me in my own little world drinking myself or smoking myself to oblivion.

I did like sports when I was younger but nothing ever lasted. I always screwed up or just didn't care any more and left. I went to two or three different schools. My parents, after trying for ages and ages, got me into a grant-maintained school called the London Nautical School, which meant me travelling from Basildon every morning to London. I hated every minute of that school. The kids were all living in London, I didn't know them, they were all bigger than me and bullied me, so I used to go into London on my Travelcard and then just head off on my own. I was twelve or thirteen. I would find myself in museums and places like that. I used to turn up at the gate and say, 'My mum and dad are in there, can I go in and find them?' and they'd just wave me through. I went to the Tower of London two or three times.

I went on jollies on my own. I had my packed lunch and my travel ticket so I could go where I wanted. That was an adventure. I can probably do a good guided tour of London now – I went everywhere.

I came out of that school and moved to a local school, but once again, I was isolated and bunked off again. When I was about fourteen I left school for good. I was a law unto myself by then. There was nothing my parents could do. I got money through stealing. Sometimes I would take money from my mum's purse or I'd steal from the changing rooms when we'd go to cricket – from people's pockets and stuff. There are eleven players on each team – that's twenty-two players, twenty-two wallets. I was a young kid, so no one was going to think it was me. If there was a couple of hundred pounds in a wallet, you'd take £40 or £50. Often I'd be dipping into people's handbags. There was always stuff lying around.

All along I was still using drugs heavily, still drinking heavily – well, I was totally out of control really. I took whatever I could get my hands on. By then I was taking speed intravenously – injecting it. I couldn't talk to anyone. I was taking these drugs and just blasting myself into space because I couldn't handle my emotions and my feelings. Nobody seemed to get on with me, nobody liked talking to me, no one was friendly with me. Instead of sitting there not being liked, a couple of spliffs later I didn't care if I wasn't liked.

I got a job at a fairground when I was eighteen, running the dodgems. The fair came to Basildon – I went on a couple of rides and asked if there was any work going. They were always taking on young lads to do the manual work, so they took me on. I travelled around with them all over the country. They didn't pay a great deal, but they used to feed you and gave you a roof over your head (we had a caravan to live in). My drug habit had gone completely out of control by now. I was on amphetamines as well as everything else – pot, strong glue. I ended up leaving the fair because I was stealing off them to buy my drugs and I got caught. If they caught you stealing, they wouldn't call the police in – they'd give you a good kicking. The police were never on the sites. So they kicked me off the fair and I ended up on the streets of Nottingham.

That was when I first found heroin. It was £10 a bag, but at first it wasn't expensive because you weren't using a lot and a £10 bag would last you two or three days. You think you're not going to get addicted but within two or three weeks it gets you. Within three or four weeks, from having a £10 bag every couple of days, it would be pretty much a bag a day, so that's £10 a day straight away. Within four or five weeks after that, you're on two bags a day, or three bags a day; you build up very, very quickly. Soon I was buying it in weight and spending hundreds of pounds each time. I was living on the streets and while I was there I was thieving and burgling and just hurting anyone who came near me. I was doing commercial burglaries – taking anything I could. There was a hairdressing salon, and while they were all working I sneaked into their tea room.

There were five or six handbags there, which meant five or six purses, five or six credit cards. Often they had their pin numbers in with their purses in case they forgot them. On a good day I'd make £2,000, £3,000, £4,000. A bad day meant I hadn't made enough to supply my habit, which meant that that night I was going to be ill. But there weren't many days when I was ill.

When I was nineteen I got caught red-handed. I can't remember what I got done for but at the end of the interview they said, 'Is there anything else you want to tell us?' and I just reeled off everything I'd done in the last six or seven months. I don't know why I did that. I never enjoyed thieving. I got two years for burglary. I hated every minute of it but it was also a relief. I was getting help for the drugs.

I had to go through cold turkey. When I turned up at the prison, I told the doctor, 'Look, I'm in bother, I'm on heroin.' At that, he threw me some paracetamol and said, 'Cold turkey never killed no one, son.' I went through a month of not sleeping – just looking at the walls. That hurt. But I could still get hold of heroin when I was in prison. My mum was sending me money and I was using it to buy drugs.

When I came out, my mum and dad were living in Mansfield and their next-door neighbour was a girl my age. She had a younger sister, and we fell in love. She got pregnant and she had my little girl, Abbie. That was in 1996. Soon I was back on heroin and crack cocaine. I was just a crazy person then. I was stealing from my girlfriend and arguing with her. I never actually hit her but I pushed her a couple of times. I was a nasty bully really. I was very good at standing over her and trying to scare her. I threatened to kill her at times. I was not a very nice person. She was right to get rid of me.

Eventually I came off heroin by Subutex at a community-based detox clinic in Nottingham recommended by my doctor. I told him I wanted to come off heroin. The cravings in my mind were ridiculous. I went to bed wanting heroin, I woke up wanting heroin and it was just too much. Even though I was off heroin and I was taking this substitute, it didn't stop me smoking heavily still and it didn't stop me drinking heavily. I was drinking five or six cans of strong lager like Tennent's Super a day, which is enough to get most people drunk, as well as smoking lots of weed and lots of other things.

I went back to heroin a couple of years later and came off it again. It was always there or thereabouts. I've had so many sort of clean times and so many dirty times. I was living in different hostels and was still stealing and in and out of prisons. I've been in about 18 different prisons. I think the biggest sentence was four years, for commercial burglaries.

In 2004 I was totally out of control. I had another girlfriend by then and my stepfather had a go at her in the house and I just flipped. I can't remember what the argument was about but my dad said a few hurtful things. My little girl was in the house that day, visiting (I used to have her at weekends). I was angry. I went upstairs and got a cricket bat out of my bedroom and came back downstairs and hit my stepfather over the head with it. I took a big swing and cut all his head open. My daughter was sitting on his lap at the time. My mum was crying, 'Why, David, why?' and I don't even know why. I just think it was years and years of anger, probably towards him for the domestic violence. Everything just flew out in one go. The police were called and I was arrested for GBH. But I got a caution for that, which is amazing because it carries a possible life sentence. I think it was because my stepfather said he didn't want to press charges. Nowadays I would be taken to court anyway, I think.

I stayed with a friend for a few nights and then I went up to Nottingham and booked myself into a bed and breakfast. It was October 2004. They call it a 'snowball' when you put heroin and crack cocaine in the same needle to inject – and that's what I did. I hadn't touched heroin for quite some time so my tolerance level was non-existent. I put it all in the needle and took the lot. When I look back, it can only have been a suicide bid, although I can't remember anything about it. That was about 10 o'clock at night. At half past ten the following morning, the hotel cleaner found me naked on the bed, unconscious. I was rushed to Queen's Medical Centre, Nottingham and put straight on a life support machine. My brother was the first there. He phoned my mum and said, 'Don't bother coming up. He isn't going to make it.'

I was on the life support machine for about a month. I had pneumonia and a minor stroke whilst in intensive care because of the lack of oxygen to the brain.

They said I was going to be brain damaged. When I woke up I can remember the doctor coming in and asking me my name and me not being able to tell him what it was. My family supported me the whole time. I've got photos of my mum feeding me, and my stepfather shaving me.

In February 2005 I walked out of hospital after being there for four months. Within three or four weeks of coming out, I was smoking pot and drinking. I joined a local cricket team, which had a lot of Pakistani Asian guys on the team, and I got quite friendly with them. I was curious about Islam. They started telling me about Allah and I started praying five times a day. I went to Dewsbury in Leeds to the mosque.

There was something eating away at me inside, I didn't feel comfortable with the Muslim faith but I needed some kind of structure in my life. I was trying to stop smoking, I was trying to stop drinking, and I just couldn't do it, so I was back on crack. I tried my hardest, but I couldn't do it. I just hoped that Allah was going to come and say 'Bang' and take all the bad stuff away from me.

By May that year I was back in prison on another two-year sentence. I was caught in the changing rooms at Lord's Cricket Ground where Middlesex were playing another county team. The police came and banged me to rights because of my past. I was sent to Belmarsh. In the prison I was attending a Muslim prayer session in the chapel about two to three months into my sentence when I sneaked off and got talking to someone from the chaplaincy team in the prison. I said, 'Look, help me, I'm a Muslim, I don't feel comfortable with this. Help me.' I picked up a Bible and the person said, 'Just read Mark's Gospel.'

That night, I read Mark's Gospel, and I read it all, which is amazing considering it was the King James Version. I read it and I was like, 'Wow, now I know what I was missing.' That night I fell on my knees and I asked God for help. It was like, 'All right, now I know you're there, Lord, help me.'

Two days after that I was transferred from Belmarsh to Brixton. I don't know why. There was no reason for them to transfer me from one prison to another but they did. Within a day of being in Brixton, I got a job down in the chapel. The vicar there at the time was a guy called Roger Green. On the Sunday, the first service was the Catholic service, so I sat in on it and loved it. Then came the Church of England service and another church came in to help lead the worship. They played some songs and stuff and I thought, 'Wow, this is amazing.'

Two days later, on the Tuesday morning, was this thing called Alpha. Roger said, 'It would be good for you to sit in on Alpha.' I started reading the books downstairs before it started and I thought, 'Ah, this is interesting.' There were about fifteen of us, all inmates. I loved it. We basically worked through the green books and someone would give a talk. Then came the session called 'What is the Holy Spirit?' We were singing a worship song and I suddenly got goose bumps all over.

I thought, 'Woah, what's that?' It felt like a jumbo jet had gone whoosh, straight over the front of me. I almost fell over when it sort of hit me like that. I thought, 'Wow.' I was overwhelmed. It knocked the hell out of me. It felt really good, but suddenly I felt really sorry – about how my life had turned out and how I had just ballsed everything up really. It was at that moment that I said a prayer. I said, 'I'm going to give you everything of mine now, Jesus. Thank you.' I gave my life to Jesus. I prayed to God, 'I want to follow you and I want to get to know you more.'

I was so sorry for everything bad I'd done in my life – my thoughts, everything. That morning there were tears rolling down my face. I was sobbing. I think the last time I cried was when I was a youngster. After that session I started praying and I didn't want to take drugs any more. I had had almost twenty years of drug abuse and isolation. It felt like it was taken from me in a second. It still really blows my mind. I was put in contact with a Christian charity called Stepping Stones, which is predominantly run from Croydon. They find you somewhere to live, they help with work and find a church for you to go to. I left prison and came to

Stepping Stones in 2006. One of the trustees invited me to the New Life Christian Centre. I got there about half past ten and the minute I walked in I felt God just said, 'Dave, you're home.' I've been there ever since. It's a fantastic church.

I go to events like Soul Survivor a lot because I like being renewed. I'm human, I'm stupid, and I still make loads and loads of mistakes. But I'm drug free and I've been drug free since 2006. I think when the Holy Spirit came into my cell that night and healed me and made me cry it took the obsession away from me. When I first came out of prison I did a drug treatment programme. I believe that Jesus gave me my heart back. I'd be dead if it wasn't for Jesus.

I want to find out what God's purpose is for me. I volunteer and help people with drug and alcohol abuse. I go out and give people advice about what's the best way to stop taking drugs. On a Friday there's a few of us that go and feed the homeless.

I have my family back now. My next step is to get myself fully up on my feet and working properly so I can go and find my daughter. It would be amazing to walk into my church with my daughter. One of the proudest things for me was when I was baptised at the church. My mum cried loads because the person they knew wasn't there any more. It blew their minds how two or three guys from the church stood up and had something to say about me.

Before the Alpha course I never knew Jesus. Now I know him. Everything bad that I've ever done in my life has gone because of that one man. I still find it really hard. I'm a Christian; I love Jesus with all my heart for what he's done for me, but forgiveness, that's the hardest one. I still struggle with that from time to time. And because I struggle with that I struggle with forgiving myself as well for my past.

I've got a real passion for reading the Bible. I've been known to go a whole day without being seen because I am in my house reading the Bible. It's God's Word, isn't it? It's amazing; I love it. I want to get married and I'd love to have more children. But the lady has to be a Christian.

There's lots of things that have happened and it all leads back to one person and that's Jesus. That's the amazing thing about it.

Dave Taylor worships at a church near his home in Croydon, where he helps at local homeless night shelters and a detox centre. He is now back in touch with his daughter, Abbie.

8 THE MUSICIAN
THE STORY OF SIMON DIXON

From his student days at the Guildhall School of Music, organist Simon Dixon's ambition was to 'make it' as a cathedral organist. He practised until his hands were raw and his feet bled. But his priorities changed. This is his story.

When I was about five, my parents bought a piano for my elder sister and every moment she wasn't on it, I wanted to be on it. I was just drawn to it. My parents let me start having lessons when I was seven. I had a lovely teacher and no one ever had to tell me to practise – I just loved it. Gradually I played more and more and won various piano prizes.

By the age of twelve I knew that music was something I wanted to do and I wanted to learn an orchestral instrument. I couldn't decide which one, so I started on the oboe, then the clarinet – but I didn't have the right mouth for either.

Then I tried the flute – but it made me dizzy! I ended up with the French horn, which I loved. I took piano and French horn to grade eight, then got a music scholarship to my senior school where I took up the organ, also to grade eight. I really struggled with the organ for the first two terms because you had to try and play without looking at your feet. But I had a very good organ teacher who invested a lot in me.

When I was seventeen, I applied to the Guildhall School of Music, who take one organist every other year. There were hundreds of people auditioning for various positions. For the organ post they narrowed it down to five of us and I was eventually accepted. I was so excited. When I started at Guildhall we were told that only 10 per cent of us would make it in the music world. So out of thirty-odd students, only three or four of us were going to 'make it' – earning our living solely from playing (instead of teaching). Although I loved teaching, I knew that wasn't what I wanted to do. I did three years at Guildhall and Harold Dexter, organist at Southwark Cathedral, taught me organ. He pushed me a lot and I learned some incredible disciplines from him. As well as being at college full time, I got an organ post at St Giles' Cripplegate in the Barbican. I made a vow that I would make it. Music was really like a god for me at that time and was where I could 'escape to'.

People talk about their mad student days, but in those three years I probably only went to the student union bar a handful of times. I didn't go out to parties; I got into a group of friends where we would spend every evening practising. I practised the organ for two to three hours every day, the piano for two hours and the French horn for about

an hour. I also had history of music, conducting, orchestra-
tion . . . Most evenings I'd be in St Giles' up in the organ
loft on my own – or practising on the organ at Guildhall. I
made my feet bleed from over-practising (I remember feeling quite pleased about that!). One time when I was in St
Giles', I got locked in all night by mistake. Most people
might be a little upset, but I remember thinking, 'This is
great – I can practise!' I think I played until about one in the
morning before falling asleep. Physically and emotionally I
would get quite run down. I didn't look after myself very
well and didn't eat well. We would give two concerts a week
at St Giles' and I was in charge of looking after all the players – on top of my full-time course. Then on Sunday mornings I led a professional choir who would be singing at
places like Glyndebourne during the week. I had to rehearse
them and it was an incredible learning experience for a
seventeen-year-old.

When I finished my degree course, my tutor suggested
doing a Masters, which I did. I don't think I've ever worked
so hard in my life as I did during my Masters year. I was
also earning my living, doing concerts, some teaching and
helping run an agency for opera singers. The lovely thing
was that, for my Masters, they offered me any teacher in
Europe I wanted. I chose Nicolas Kynaston, who had been
an organist for ten years at Westminster Cathedral, and
whose playing I admired hugely. So I had some very happy
lessons with him. I went flat out. I did my dissertation on
French organ music and my thesis on J. S. Bach and passed
the Masters, which was a great relief. I continued working
and practising and working and practising.

As an organist in this country, the pinnacle of one's career is to become a cathedral organist. But the opportunities to be a cathedral organist are few and far between. Your first port of call would be to become a sub organist. These jobs are nearly always appointed through word-of-mouth recommendation – but I was from completely the wrong background for a cathedral because nearly all the organists who got these places were Oxbridge organ scholars. So I never really expected to have that opportunity.

Life for the next ten years involved playing concerts. I was invited to play in America to audiences of organists and to teach master classes in Oxford and Cambridge to organ scholars. I played concerts in St Paul's, Winchester, Leicester, Manchester and Chichester Cathedrals and at the Albert Hall during the Last Night of the Proms. That was an amazing experience. I remember people singing so loudly I couldn't hear myself playing. I played in France, Germany, Spain, Holland, Portugal, Slovakia, America, New Zealand and Canada. Sometimes alone, sometimes for a choir or orchestra. I played in all these churches but I wasn't a churchgoer. In fact, church was the last place I wanted to go. They were usually cold, rather unfriendly places. By the age of twenty-six or twenty-seven, I felt I'd 'made it'. I had a beautiful home by Hammersmith Bridge and a sports car. I worked very hard. Concerts brought in money and I made recordings, I conducted, I sang, I accompanied, I taught, I worked with an agency. Despite achieving everything I had worked so hard for, I realised that I was still searching for something that I hadn't yet found.

Then, in 1989 some great friends of mine, David and Jo Loveless, invited me to a Billy Graham crusade at Earl's Court Arena. We got there and there were hundreds of people in the choir. I remember being incredibly impressed by the music and the numbers of young people. When Billy Graham spoke it felt as if he was talking just to me. He said, 'Jesus is at the door knocking to come into your life. The handle is on the inside and you are the one that has to open it.' At the end they asked if people wanted to give their lives to God. I said to my friends, 'I think I'll go down and find out a bit more.' As I went down the staircase I said, very clumsily, 'Jesus, if you are there, I am sorry I have ignored you all my life. Please forgive me for the things I have done wrong, and I ask you to come into my life.'

At that moment, I felt this heat flood through me, and this overwhelming sensation in my heart and my whole body. I just wept and wept. Some people came and prayed with me and I felt God speak to me. It was the sense that I could only worship one God and he was asking me to give him my music, which I had held onto so tightly my whole life. In my prayers I said I was willing never to do music again and to worship God alone. That is what was genuinely on my heart in that moment. So I became a Christian that Thursday night. I tried to think of a church to go to and remembered this link with Holy Trinity Brompton. I had visited the church as a schoolboy and had kept in touch with Paul Joslin, the organist, and had sung a couple of times in the choir. So I started attending there on Sundays.

Then I went on Alpha, which was just wonderful for me. It put meat on the bones and answered the questions that I needed to ask – things I was embarrassed to find I didn't know, despite being in church all my life. I made some good friends and joined a prayer group and a pastorate. Becoming a Christian affected my music hugely. Overnight my ambition and drive changed, which freed up my playing – it was better! It was now for God and not for me.

Soon afterwards, my organ teacher said, 'I have been asked to recommend somebody to a well-known London cathedral and I would like to recommend you.' On the same day, Sandy Millar, [former] Vicar of Holy Trinity Brompton, asked me if I would consider helping out on a part-time basis. It was so lovely of God to show me that possibly I was good enough to go for a big cathedral position – but I had absolutely no doubt what I had to do. At the cathedral, I would have worked incredibly hard but would have been miserable. It would have become my whole life. But HTB was home. There was absolutely no question in my mind but to accept Sandy's offer. I don't think Sandy quite realised that he was asking me to say goodbye to this life, my career. I knew that once I took the post at HTB that would be the end of my career. The invitations would dry up quickly. After all, what sort of professional organist would work at a church that has guitars? But I took it like a shot and I trusted God for how I was going to earn my living. My only worry was, 'How am I going to play from chord sheets?'

The worship leaders were so patient with me. We learned together as we gradually incorporated the organ with the worship band. I had to pay the bills, so I built up a network marketing business selling water filters.

Sandy's vision was to have excellent music from within the body of the church. He recognised that there were many gifted people within the church – people who needed to be encouraged – and that we should welcome these church members to worship God through music. There were so many excellent musicians at HTB, including the wonderful Jo and José-Luis Garcia (he was the principal leader of the English Chamber Orchestra for many years and Jo also played in the orchestra). In fact, we are now involving some musicians from within the parish, Imperial College and the Royal College of Music. We started a chamber choir and it was great fun. I started to realise that through letting go of everything and joining in with the choruses and with the band during services, God was gradually using and restoring all the gifts he had given me, and all my training was being put to good use.

After a few years, Sandy invited me to join the staff full time and it felt right. We started developing three classical concerts, all involving HTB congregations. So we were able to implement Sandy's vision. The Christmas carol service – with a large and wonderful choir and orchestra – became two services, then three, then four. I did thirteen carol services last Christmas (at Tollington Park, Harrods, the Brompton Hospital, Christingle, etc.) – all within our community, which you could say was almost too much of a good thing! Somebody who didn't know me once said to me, 'Isn't HTB where they have that wonderful classical music?' And I have to admit I said silently, 'Oh thank you, Lord.' There are some people who only come to the classical or carol concerts. You wouldn't get them to church services, but my prayer is that they might then consider coming on an Alpha course at some point in the future.

I have played at hundreds of weddings now. A typical HTB wedding would be organ, band and maybe a classical piece. The standard of musicianship is incredibly high – we want to give people our very best. I was getting a little bit frustrated at still being single as I hit my 500th wedding, and had gone off travelling during my sabbatical.

When I came back in September 2001 I met Caryn at our first ever Worship Conference at Holy Trinity. I looked up, saw her and thought, 'There you are . . .' I think I knew in that moment that we were going to get married. Caryn had been leading worship in her pastorate so she came to my talk at the Worship Conference on 'Performance to Praise' – my testimony about how I came from performing to worshipping God. She auditioned for the worship choir (and got in on merit!) and then joined the Christmas Choir. We fell in love and I asked her to marry me on New Year's Eve 2002. We got married in June 2003 at HTB. Sandy married us and we had a wonderful wedding with all our families, friends, and some amazing music.

I feel that God has literally plucked me out of darkness, and I know I wouldn't be here today if it wasn't for him.

In 2010 Simon Dixon was appointed Director of Worship at the Falls Church in Washington DC, USA. In recognition of his achievements in church music, he was awarded the St Mellitus Medal by the Bishop of London in the same year.

9 THE SECURITY GUARD
THE STORY OF BILLY GILVEAR

After embarking on an army career, Billy Gilvear became a security guard to celebrities including Take That, Adam Clayton and Mel Gibson. But the hedonistic life-style brought him to the edge of destruction.

My father was a Glasgow gangster, brought up in the Gorbals in the east end of Glasgow. He ran with a notorious gang and a few of his gang mates were hanged for murder. When he was still a teenager, he went to a tent mission in Glasgow and became a Christian. From that day his life was completely transformed. He eventually became a missionary in Africa. I was one year old when my mum and dad returned from Africa to live in Glasgow. My dad started working as a full-time evangelist and preached all over.

Growing up I was very sporty, full of life and extremely rebellious. I decided there was no God and this gospel that my dad preached was just a fantasy. Some Sundays we would be on the road with Dad. If he was preaching at a church – Wee Free [Free Church of Scotland], Brethren, Pentecostal, Presbyterian – we would be invited as a family. When we weren't in church we had to stay in – it was the Lord's Day. We couldn't even go out and kick a ball. Instead we had to stay indoors and listen to Cliff Richard records.

I always disagreed with Christian principles, therefore we would argue a lot and home became a battlefield. I hated the church, Christianity, God and Jesus. I didn't feel I was given any freedom. I just saw restriction. I knew from a young age that I wanted to leave home and go into the army. By the age of sixteen I had completed all my army medical, physical and aptitude tests, and on 6 January 1986 I left home. I thought it was fantastic.

As I stepped onto the bus to leave home that day, my dad said, 'You're going to take this with you,' and handed me a Bible. I looked at it and said, 'No.' That was a very symbolic moment. My father was devastated when I left.

By this time I was angry, furious and very physical – and as a junior leader in the army I had one of the best years of my life. I'd say, 'This is easier than home.'

But it was brutal. In those days they still had a lot of bullying in the army. I remember three days into the army falling asleep in a lecture on biological chemical warfare. The corporal giving the lecture grabbed a rifle by the muzzle and stood above me, then whacked the barrel down on top of my head at full speed. It cracked my head open but he kept kicking me brutally and said, 'Don't you ever fall asleep in one of my lectures again!' I went over to the medical centre and got a couple of stitches in the head, then went back to the barracks to carry on. But I didn't mind. I knew it was going to be brutal and physical. I graduated as the top junior leader from my year. My dad came to the graduation and passing out parade. It was a very proud moment for me, because I knew I had succeeded without God.

Then I was put on fast track promotion. By eighteen I had joined the First Battalion, Argyle and Southern Highlanders – that was my regiment – and soon afterwards my commanding officer called me into his office and said, 'We believe you'd make a good officer.' In those days officers came from universities or your father had a big name in the City or owned Lloyds or whatever. You didn't come from the ranks of the Scottish regiments. I was the first junior rank from the Argyles to go forward for commission. They put me forward to do a three-month Potential Officer Development Course at Beaconsfield. We were given etiquette lessons on how to hold a wine glass and what was the appropriate drink before the appropriate meat. We went up to the operas in London and had to listen to classical music.

It was during this course that I met Bev. Bev was a full corporal working in the stores there. She issued me a sleeping bag and then I noticed her at various points through the camp. Within three months we were engaged to be married. Because I was at Sandhurst training to become an officer, Bev decided to give up her job in the army. She was a corporal and it wouldn't have been compatible to marry an officer. We would never have seen each other. We had booked a church wedding – the great day that Bev had always wanted. But then a few months before, I decided I didn't want to get married and certainly not in a church. I was scared of the commitment and feared Bev would get in the way of my plans for the future. When I told her I didn't want to get married she was devastated, obviously. We had to cancel everything and let the 200 guests know.

Then, about two days later, I knew I'd made a huge mistake. Bev took me back but it wasn't the same. Our original wedding had been booked for September, but we ended up getting married in November in a registry office in Pontypool, near Bev's family home. Bev's family and friends came but my family from Scotland didn't come – they thought it was all a bad idea. Everyone was naturally very disappointed and angry with me. At Sandhurst I met seriously wealthy guys with fathers who owned half of Berkshire. I remember one time we saw one guy's father's house and it was like this castle in the country. All my time there I had to be the best – I was an all or nothing guy. There was something in me that had to succeed. I felt so good when my sergeant major or commanding officer said, 'Well done, Gilvear!'

But there was always a void in me no matter what I achieved. I'd always be wanting to move on to the next thing. So, soon after Sandhurst with an amazing career in front of me, I left the army. I felt that I could earn more money as a civilian. Bev was devastated because she had left the army in order to marry me – and now I was walking out of it. My new job was in the world of private security – looking after A-list celebrities from the film and music industry. The money was good and several other soldiers left the army to do it.

My main contract was with Take That, but we also looked after The Bee Gees, Adam Clayton from U2 (he was dating Naomi Campbell at the time), Mel Gibson and his wife, Arnold Schwarzenegger, Sylvester Stallone and many more. I was their close protection bodyguard, which meant you lived with them. Wherever they went, you went with them and would look after their security needs. If there were no pictures to be taken, you would make sure no pictures were taken. I found it really exciting to be moving in this new glamorous world.

We went on tour with Take That. We would ensure that nobody who they didn't want near them got near them, that they got from hotel to venue safely and vice versa. If they went out socialising you went with them to protect them. This was at the height of Take That fame, when Robbie Williams was in the band. It was absolute madness – the female fans were just obsessed. You'd get these fifteen-year-old girls scratching your eyeballs out to get to the boys. Without us, the boys would have been torn apart. We were protecting them from all sorts of weird and wonderful people really. It was at this point in my life that I really thought I'd arrived. I thought, 'I've got this great job with these really glamorous people . . .' and we got paid very well.

By this time Jordan, our son, had been born (in 1993). But I wasn't seeing much of my family because of work. It was so bad that soon after Jordan was born, Bev moved out of our home back to Wales to be close to her family. My life had already started to become very hedonistic. Working so close to the celebrities, I joined in the celebrity lifestyle, living life in the fast lane, going to all the parties. When our clients were sleeping we were still working, taking shifts. So we got very little sleep. We worked morning, noon and night. When I wasn't working, I was partying hard.

This was the first point in my life where I was introduced to drugs. At the centre of the music industry there is a big drug culture. Ecstasy was becoming massive on the scene and cocaine was 'the drug'. At one party I attended there were little bowls full of cocaine – it was just help yourself. That was the world we were in. The lifestyle is 100-miles-an-hour – really intensive.

I was a real social guy anyway and loved a good heavy drinking session. Alcohol was very much part of my life in the army. When I wasn't working, I would take cocaine and Ecstasy, but not alcohol because you couldn't drive with alcohol. I stacked Ecstasy and cocaine together – that was the biggest hit. When I wasn't driving I would drink too.

For me it was as though Bev didn't exist. I was really horrible to her through those years. I was glad that she'd gone back to Wales because I knew she was being looked after by her family. It meant that I could get on with my life without feeling so guilty. I'd join her in Wales occasionally and spend some time there.

By the time we had our second son, Jack, in 1995, the drugs had really taken hold of my life. The cocaine and Ecstasy were no longer giving me the buzz I got at the start, so I was having to take more Es to get the same hit that I got the first time.

Everyone knew about my drug addiction – including my parents and Bev. It was no secret. I would do what every addict does and say, 'No, I've got it under control,' but I knew I couldn't deal with it. The security company gave me chance after chance to stop but I couldn't. I started to do a bit of drug dealing, getting to know some of the gangster element who were bringing the drugs in. That was when I was given the sack.

After that, I was hanging on for dear life. Cocaine and Ecstasy were no longer enough, so I progressed on to crack. The first time I had a smoke of the pipe I had the most intense hit I've ever had in my life. You can't describe it. That was it really – the point of no return. At that point I recognised that I had destroyed my life. I was filled with guilt, remorse and pain. I thought, 'What have I done?' I knew I'd hurt so many people, done so many wrong things. I went back to Scotland to visit my parents and it was there that I attempted suicide with an overdose of paracetamol and alcohol. My youngest sister and my mum found me semi-conscious in the dining room. They knew there was something wrong so they took me to hospital. At the hospital they pumped my stomach and then they put me into a recovery ward overnight. I remember coming round early in the morning and seeing my mum rubbing the back of my hand. I was on a drip and the needle was quite painful and she kept hitting it as she rubbed my hand.

I was probably at the lowest point in my life and she whispered in my ear, 'Billy, I've got to tell you this. God still loves you and he's told me that one day you're going to preach the gospel. I know you don't want to hear that but . . .' And then she just prayed for me and carried on rubbing my hand. It was an amazing moment. From there they put me into a psychiatric hospital.

I went through cold turkey, which was horrendous. They gave me good medication, but I was still bad. My family would visit me and my sister would sometimes come and take me out for a meal at KFC. But I felt pretty rubbish about myself.

After a while I went back to Wales. Bev took me back out of sympathy and for the sake of the boys. But within a few months I was back on drugs in Wales. I was horrible to Bev. I used to rob her – she'd budget for the kids and I'd take that money. I'd take all the money she had and spend it on drugs. I'd become this real scumbag, a really disgusting person. This was 1999–2000. I would go away for days on end on drug-induced binges and I'd come back from the gutter. This wasn't about having fun – I was an addict and I hated myself. Finally there came a point when Bev had to cut me out of her life for the sake of the children. She said, 'I can't do this any more, you can't come here any more.' And she asked for a divorce.

Around this time I was charged with grievous bodily harm after I assaulted a guy at a party. We had a disagreement when I asked him for a light for my cigarette – and I absolutely flipped. I broke his jaw, his cheekbone, his nose and cut his eyes. He had to have a plate put in to set his cheek back in place. I didn't know how much damage I'd done until the next day when I was arrested. Apparently he could hardly breathe – he was in a bad way. In the end I was very lucky not to go to prison. After leaving court I realised how bad things had got. I'd hurt my wife, my children, my parents, people who loved me. What's more, I was dangerous.

Some time later, I was drinking in a local pub when this guy I knew came in and said, 'My brother needs someone to help him on the farm. Do you want the job?' He knew I needed some cash – and there was accommodation with the job. So I accepted. The farm was about four miles from Bev's home. When I walked into the kitchen I saw all these Alpha course posters and Christian pictures. I thought, 'What on earth is this?' My friend said, 'I meant to tell you, mate, my mum's a Christian. She'll be all right – she won't bother you.'

It turned out that his mum Nancy was the most fanatical Christian you'd ever met in your life. Not only that, the farm was used for Alpha Holy Spirit weekends for all the churches in South Wales. I thought, 'I'm trying to run away from this God thing, and here I am walking right into it . . .!'

I was still on drugs but not as intensively, because I was also on medication. So I was kind of in a better place. But I was still drinking a lot of alcohol – getting drunk every night. I could drink whole bottles of whisky and still stay sober. Whisky was my drink.

To get to my bedroom I had to go through the kitchen, where the Alpha groups would be having their meals, and through the lounge, where they would be having their ministry time. I found out later that Nancy was always telling these churches who came, 'You need to pray for Billy, he's a recovering addict. He's up in his room and his life's a mess, he's gone through a divorce . . .'

But some of these churches were so fanatical that if they saw me they would land on me and start praying out loud for me. If I didn't make it to the stairs in time they'd pounce on me and start praying in turns over me.

I totally resisted it all – I just wasn't getting it. It was probably the loneliest time of my life on that farm. I used to hate waking up in the morning because I just wanted to die in my sleep. I'd think of my sons and Bev a few miles away . . . It was horrible.

Then on the news I heard about someone who had committed suicide. He had researched on a suicide page on the internet how to kill himself. So I went to the local library in Newport and looked on the computer to find out how to do it. For me, this was all or nothing. On the farm we had a big silage tank and one day we were cleaning it out. I had to climb up the ladders on the side and I looked inside and saw these huge metal hooks. I don't know what the hooks were for, but I thought, 'That's what I'll do.'

So I prepared my suicide. I researched the noose knot and how that worked and I'd set everything in place to hang myself. It was going to happen the weekend before my 30th birthday. I was like the walking dead – lifeless. My heart burned so much my body was painful. I got out of bed on 6 December 2000 and went down into the kitchen.

There I found Nancy cleaning all her brass utensils. She was holding an old brass kettle in her hand, which was covered in black grime. She covered it with polish and as she was rubbing it, it came up sparkling clean. All of a sudden I was transfixed by this pot and I felt like somebody was saying to me, 'Billy, this is your life.' It was like an audible voice. Twice I heard it.

Then all of a sudden all these verses that I'd memorised unwillingly as a child started coming back: 'Jesus said, "I am the way, the truth, and the life."

"I have come that they may have life and have it to the full." '

Then I thought of John 3:16: 'For God so loved the world, that he gave his only begotten Son, that whosoever believeth in him should not perish, but have everlasting life' (KJV). It all came flooding back. I remembered this black heart that my mum used for her Bible Club where she did children's talks. She stuck a red velvet cross on it. The black heart represented my sin and the red cross represented Jesus dying on the cross. Then she had this white heart – white because of what Jesus had done on the cross for us. Our hearts, our lives, everything could be clean. All this came to me in moments.

And I realised that I'd just heard from God. He was saying, 'Look, Billy, you still have a chance, if you give your life back to me.' I knew he could clean my life up until it sparkled like that pot. That morning I went out with Rob to lay some turf on this new building site and I looked up to the sky and said, 'God, if that was you, you've got to help me. I'm sorry for the things that I've done . . . but God, I've got nothing left.'

I was really desperate. I'll never forget it. It was a freezing morning, but beautiful with sunshine. All of a sudden all the drugs and everything in my system started to leave my body – downwards, from head down. Everything started to drift away and I remember feeling this amazing peace that I'd never felt before. And then it felt like somebody was giving me a hug, saying, 'It's going to be all right.' Then came this amazing feeling of joy. As I stood in that garden my life was absolutely devastated, yet I felt a happiness that I'd never, ever experienced – not even on drugs.

I thought, 'Whoa. What is that?' By now I had an amazing smile – the emptiness, the void, the hunger was beginning to get filled. I felt cosy and warm – I started to feel alive. I was looking at the sky and at the greenery around me, and it was like I hadn't seen it before. I turned round and Rob said, 'What's that on your face? I've never seen you smile like that.'

I said quietly, 'Jesus, thank you. Not only can I feel you, but these people can see you. Now I know you're alive.'

That night I told Nancy what had happened to me and she prayed for me there and then. Then I phoned my dad. I said, 'Dad, I've something to tell you. Today I gave my heart to Jesus.' There was silence on the phone and then an amazing celebration. My mum was hysterical and crying and we were all rejoicing, because they had waited thirty years. Then I found this Baptist church and I went there on the Sunday. I still wasn't making much sense of what had happened, but I knew I was transformed.

I told everyone. I had already stopped the drugs and alcohol. It was miraculous. A couple of weeks later I stopped smoking. God knew for me it was all or nothing – I couldn't have done it halfway or gradually. I was at the end of my tether and God knew it and so he did it.

I then did an Alpha course that was being run on the farm by Nancy and some of her friends. We heard the talks on video with Nicky Gumbel. We had a Holy Spirit day on the farm. There were about six of us. During the prayer ministry time this old lady prayed for me to receive the Holy Spirit and it was amazing. I was crying. Then somebody started laughing and we all went down in absolute hysterics – from tears into laughter. I continued on Alpha and I loved it.

Bev had become a Christian nine months earlier. My parents had been praying for her and my mum had sent her a book on hope. Bev had read it and given her heart to the Lord.

Four months after I became a Christian – Easter Sunday 2001 – was my baptism. Bev, my boys, my parents and my sisters came. I shared my testimony and I said, 'I was once lost but now I'm found. I was blind, but now I see.' As I said, 'Now I see,' Bev told me afterwards that God spoke to her and said, 'You can love this man again.' After the baptism she came over, hugged me and said, 'I need to speak to you tomorrow.' I went over to her house and she said, 'God told me last night that I could love you again.' That year we started courting and a year later we were remarried in the local Baptist church. We had the reception in one of the barns on the farm. We had a barn dance and a celebration. My parents, my sons, and lots of my friends were there. It was the special wedding day that Bev had always wanted. I got my wife back, I got my sons back, I got my life back.

In 2001, just before we remarried, I got connected with a church in Cardiff, Rubina Baptist. It's a big church that works with the students of Cardiff. They invited me to help on their Alpha course, which they were running in a really cool wine bar. It was an amazing venue – really funky with live music – the best venue that I've ever done an Alpha in. I loved it.

I asked them, 'What do you want me to do?'

They said, 'You can do the talks.'

I said, 'I can't do the talks.'

They said, 'You do the talks, man. It's OK, we're going to go to a conference first.' So we went to an Alpha for Students conference at Holy Trinity Brompton in London and it just blew me away. The whole place was oozing Jesus. I met some amazing people and the talks were great. I got prayed for by Sandy Millar during the ministry time. I really got the vision. And then we went back and ran a Student Alpha. We saw students saved through the course.

I did all the talks bar three. What I didn't realise was that through doing the talks on Alpha I was being prepared for ministry. I was doing the very thing that my mum had said I would do – preach the gospel. Just before we got married the minister came to me and said, 'We believe God's calling you into ministry.' So we tested that call and looked at some colleges and people prayed for us. God opened some doors and we found a way into Spurgeon's College where I studied theology for five years. After finishing training, I was given a job leading a church on the Channel Island of Guernsey. Not only that, but three days after arriving in Guernsey, I got a part-time job as the senior chaplain in Guernsey Prison. We are starting an Alpha course in the prison very soon.

Bev and I have had two more children since remarrying – Ben and Lydia. My life has been transformed. We weren't a family before – it was very dysfunctional. Now we're a whole family, functional and full of life.

Before all this happened to me, I thought Jesus was just a figment of my parents' imagination. But now he is the reason that I live. He's the reason that my family are together. I talk to him every day. He's my hero.

10 THE ARMED ROBBER
THE STORY OF DAMIAN MCGUINNESS

Brought up by a single mother and an alcoholic step-father on a Manchester council estate, Damian McGuinness quickly became involved in street crime – stealing cars, burglary and assault. Then things escalated when he was arrested for armed robbery and sentenced to six years in prison. Here he describes how God spoke to him in a remarkable night-time encounter in his cell – and how, gradually, that experience sparked the beginning of a total change in his life.

My dad walked out when I was about three. Four years later my mum got involved with a bloke who turned out to be a violent alcoholic. We called him our stepdad but they never married. Once he arrived on the scene, things weren't too good. He was drunk all the time, always arguing and being mean to my mum and us. When he was drunk he beat up my mum and us. We were always scared, wondering when he was going to get mad. My mum stuck with him because she felt sorry for him.

I became a bit of a bully at school and used to get into fights. The thing that escalated for me was the alcohol. From about age fourteen or fifteen I drank whatever I could get my hands on – usually cheap cider or strong lager. I'd get absolutely hammered all the time. I started getting into fights with other gangs – mainly school gangs.

When I was fifteen I broke into some offices. I broke the window, climbed in and stole the computers because I wanted a computer. I got caught but I didn't go to prison because I was too young. That was my first offence.

After leaving school I had two really mad years of drink, drugs and fighting. My life was out of control. I couldn't hold a job down because I was drinking so much all the time. I ended up going to live with my nanna. I had a little cupboard under the stairs where I slept. I'd get drunk in there. My nanna didn't mind because I was her favourite. I used to get away with murder.

When I got drunk I'd do stupid things like steal cars. I thought, 'If you want respect, it's good to get in trouble with the police.' I was never a successful car thief. I got arrested for two car thefts, a couple of drunk and disorderly and a couple of assaults. I also got into trouble for resisting arrest – that's when the police try to put you in their van and you start fighting with them.

My mate had this imitation firearm that could fire blank bullets. It just made a loud bang. One day we were really stoned after smoking weed – and really drunk. We started messing about with the gun in the fields. Later we were walking along the main road, past a takeaway restaurant, when I said to my mate, 'I'll show you how to do an armed robbery.' So I ran into the shop and started shooting the gun at the guys behind the counter. I couldn't have hurt them, but they weren't to know that. They ran out of the back of the shop screaming. Then I emptied the till. As I was leaving the shop, there was a policeman going past. Somebody had heard us firing the gun in the fields and had called the police. We got chased down the road by the police car. They must have radioed for backup because there were helicopters, police dogs, an armed response, everything. It quickly became a massive deal.

We ran down into this cul-de-sac and my mate jumped into a bin to hide while I hid in some bushes. The police followed and shouted, 'We're going to send a dog in.' Immediately, I said, 'Don't send the dog in – I'll come out to you.' So I came out.

I thought I'd get charged for being drunk and disorderly, but the police said, 'Oh no, we've got you this time. You're looking at ten to fifteen years.'

I said, 'No way, man.'

That was July 1998. I was eighteen.

That October I went to court. I pleaded guilty and the judge said, 'Six years – send him down.' I couldn't believe it.

The first thing I noticed when I went to prison is that I wasn't as tough as I thought I was. Because of the way I'd grown up, I knew that the best form of defence was to act tough so that nobody would mess with you again. But deep down inside, I was still just a scared little boy. I started at Hindley Young Offenders Institution and it was awful. I remember on the first day seeing this young lad from Newcastle. He was standing outside the office crying, with no shoes on because someone had stolen his trainers in the exercise yard. I thought, 'This is absolute hell.'

Prison broke me as a person – it broke my hard heart. In Hindley we got an hour's 'association' – where you get out of your cell to talk to the other inmates – and an hour's exercise. But the rest of the time you're in your cell so you get a lot of time to think.

I'd never really been to church as a child. My mum and stepdad never went. But in Hindley there was a chapel class on Tuesday nights and I thought I'd go along for an hour or so to see other people. It was run by two guys who came in from a church in Manchester somewhere. The two guys were Jed and Cossie (his nickname) – and they were really down-to-earth, normal people.

I'd never met anyone like them. I expected them to be geeky and soft but these guys weren't. They just loved Jesus. I was shocked.

They and their team had grown up in the inner city and some of them had struggled with drink and drugs. They'd given their life to Jesus and Jesus had set them free. They were really on fire for God. There were about fifteen of us young offenders in a room with two or three of these evangelical, wacky kind of Christians. Sometimes they would look at a Bible passage and other times they would talk about how they became Christians. I was interested and started to listen. I really needed a miracle, because I was in a bad way. I went to these chapel classes for maybe two months before I got shipped out to another prison.

At my last session, Cossie ended by saying, 'I'm going to pray . . .' And he began to pray for us as a group. As he prayed, this atmosphere just descended on the room. I looked round and every single person in the room was sitting there, hands joined together, eyes closed, reverent, just showing respect while this guy prayed. I couldn't believe that nobody else was looking around. I watched Cossie as he was praying and I thought, 'Where is this guy getting these words from?' His prayer was like this beautiful, eloquent throb. He was freestyling, pouring his heart out to God in a way that I didn't know. I had been to a Catholic school and I was used to scripted prayers like 'Our Father' and 'Hail Mary' – but this guy was talking to God, really pouring out his heart.

I thought, 'That's the Holy Spirit.' And in my heart I said, 'God, I want what he's got.' He just had this look of peace on his face as he poured his heart out to his Father.

That night, as I dozed off in my cell, I suddenly saw this light coming towards me that scared me awake. I realised that if it carried on coming towards me it would hit me so I woke up. I was shocked and thought, 'What was that? What was that?'

Then into my mind came the words: 'Romans, chapter ten, verse eight.' I didn't understand it. No one had ever said anything like that to me before. I kept a little blue Gideon's Bible under the table in my cell, so I got out of bed and found it. I opened it randomly and – bang – it opened immediately on Romans chapter ten.

I thought, 'This is weird . . .' Then I started getting goose pimples on the back of my neck. I read down a few verses.

Verse eight said: 'The word is near you; it is in your mouth and in your heart, that is, the message concerning faith that we proclaim.'

Then I read verse nine which said, 'if you confess with your mouth, "Jesus is Lord," and believe in your heart that God raised him from the dead, you will be saved.'

So I said, 'OK, Jesus is Lord.' At once I was filled with a rush from the soles of my feet, up my back and into my head. Within a short time, I was dancing around my cell. I'd been touched by God. It was the most amazing experience ever.

Nobody could tell me after that that God wasn't real.

That was November 1998 – just four or five months into my sentence, and just after I was sentenced to six years. I didn't get the chance to share this experience with anybody, because the next day I got shipped out to Castington Prison in Northumberland. I couldn't even tell Cossie.

Castington Prison was the worst place I'd ever been to in my life. It was absolutely horrific. It was north of Newcastle and it was full of Geordies. If you were a Mancunian it was the worst place you could get sent to because of regional animosity. The first thing I did when I got there was say to God, 'God, I need to do something about this experience you've given me. What should I do?'

So I opened my Gideon's Bible (which I'd brought with me) for guidance and it opened bang at Galatians, chapter six, verse six.

The verse jumped out at me: 'The one who receives instruction in the word should share all good things with their instructor.'

Once a month after chapel at Hindley, I'd been given religious instruction by Father John, the Catholic chaplain. So after reading that verse I wrote to Father John to let him know what had happened. He wrote back saying, 'That's amazing. God really wants to become special friends with you.' He ended up discipling me by mail.

There was a chapel at Castington and it was great. I started going every Sunday and I loved it. Although prison life was harder up in Northumberland, going to chapel was a lot easier. Often other inmates would take the mickey out of you and make comments if you were lining up to go to chapel. However, in Castington there was quite a large Irish community who had a genuine faith. They were also quite hard so nobody took the mickey out of me for going to chapel.

I started praying and reading the Bible – I was hungry for God. I knew I was in a rubbish place, but I knew that God was with me. It was a new and exciting time for me.

I spent about eighteen months in Castington. I got bullied there – intimidated. The servers at mealtimes would always give more food to the Geordies, and sometimes they would spit in our food. I didn't really like to eat anything.

I came out of jail in August 2001. I was met at the gates by my mum, my sister and one of my brothers. My stepdad wasn't there – he had committed suicide while I was inside. It was a wonderful day but there was this big knot of worry in my stomach all the time. I couldn't believe I was really getting released.

On my first day out of prison, I went home to my mum's and met my sister's new boyfriend. The first thing he said was, 'Shall we go out for a drink to celebrate?' I knew all about the dangers of alcohol but I went out with him for a drink and got drunk. It was the start of a big, big dip.

I started drinking and getting drunk again pretty much every night. I met up again with all my friends who were now taking cocaine and Ecstasy and stuff like that – quite hard drugs. I had a job in a warehouse but when I got home I'd smoke weed, drink beer and take cocaine. At weekends I would stay up taking Ecstasy from Friday till Sunday – non-stop partying. One weekend I'd just got my monthly wage and I spent it in one weekend on coke. That's how bad I was.

I wasn't going to church any more. When I'd first got out of prison I had wanted to carry on with my faith and went to a few churches, but there was nothing there. I just found it really difficult. From August to January it was just reckless partying and taking lots of coke and Ecstasy.

I lost my job over Christmas because I took a big bag of Ecstasy to the Christmas party and had about ten pills myself. I went wild. So I found myself with no job, no money and drinking cheap cider. I was at an all-time low with no self-esteem, no respect at all. I was totally messed up.

One day soon after that I was at home alone watching daytime TV, and I looked around at the mess in the house. There were piles of paper everywhere and for some reason I decided to tidy up. So I started chucking all this stuff out and then suddenly I saw this leaflet among all my mum's papers. It was a leaflet for a church called North Manchester Family Church. I thought, 'Where's this church then? I've never heard of it.'

On the back of the leaflet there was an advert for the Alpha course. I'd heard of Alpha because when I was in prison and going on with God, I read a book in my cell called *The God Who Changes Lives*. I'd found the book in the prison library and it was full of how the Holy Spirit had come in amazing power and changed people's lives. Most of the people had been on an Alpha course and I'd thought at the time, 'I'd love to be part of something like that.'

So now I looked at the leaflet and decided to phone the Alpha course number. I phoned them up and said, 'I hear you run an Alpha course – do you mind if I come along?' They went, 'Well, we're in week three at the moment, but I think it'll be OK if you come along.' I said, 'Do you mind if I just come and see what your church is like?' They said it was fine and the following Sunday I turned up at the school hall where they met.

I'd had a heavy night the night before and walked in with a five-day stubble and a bit of a hangover. Immediately, a girl came up to me and said, 'Hi, how are you?' The church was full of young people and there was a full worship band with drum kit, electric guitar, bass guitars. The place was just full of life. I looked around and thought, 'Wow, this is amazing. This is something I want to be a part of.'

So I turned up on Alpha a couple of days later. The course was led by a man called Howard Kellet in the front room of his house. There were about eight of us in total. When I came out of prison everyone in my social circle was dealing drugs and drinking. But through Alpha I was intro-duced to a different social circle. It was difficult to break away from what I was into – drink and drugs – but I kept going to Alpha anyway. Then, a few weeks later, at one Alpha session, Howard changed the programme.

He said, 'We were supposed to be doing the talk for week six about such and such . . . but I was praying before I started and I'm just going to tell you about the prodigal son.' He read the story of the prodigal son from the Bible, then gave his testimony about how he had been a prodigal son.

I knew he was talking to me. I knew I was the prodigal son and God was asking me to come back to him. At the end of his talk he asked, 'Does anybody want to give their life to Jesus?' And I said to one of the helpers, 'Listen, man, I'm not leaving here tonight until I give my life to Jesus. I really want to do it.' I knew that night that I had to make a conscious decision to give my life to Jesus. God spoke to me clearly through the prodigal son.

So that night I gave my life to Jesus. It was 5 March 2002. From that moment on it was a slow and long journey out of darkness with many slips. But I was on my way back to God.

I didn't quite make it to the Alpha Day for some reason. I fell away for a week or two. I was like a pendulum swing-ing between the two – it was really hard. When the next Alpha course came round the church suggested I come on it, because I'd missed the first three weeks plus some other sessions of the first course. So I did Alpha again.

This time it was better, because I was doing it as some-one who was committed. I was also helping out on it, sharing my experiences with people. So it was really good. On the Holy Spirit Sunday they said, 'If anybody wants to receive the Holy Spirit, then come to the front now.' I sat there thinking, 'Go on, go on, go on . . .' I got the courage to go to the front and three people laid hands on me and prayed for me.

They prayed for me to receive the Holy Spirit and I was saying, 'No, no, no . . .' I didn't want to make an emotional response or just mimic other people as they prayed in tongues. I didn't receive the Holy Spirit that day and I said to God, 'I'm leaving.' So I left church that day with a firm resolve not to go back.

On the Monday I went out with my old mates. We drove into the countryside to this park and set up a tent. Then we got drunk and smoked weed in the tent – it was all filled up with smoke. We got hammered.

On our way back home my mate stopped off at the chippy to get some supper. So I was sat in the car on my own. As I was sitting there I felt something come into the car – it felt as if God had removed the front windscreen of the car and just imparted the Holy Spirit to me.

As he did so, I began to speak in tongues. I had sobered up straight away – I knew it wasn't the drugs. I'd been in God's presence before, in jail, so I knew what it felt like. God was in the car with me and no one can tell me any different. Satan might tell me it was the drugs or drink. But I know I received the Holy Spirit that night.

When God or the Holy Spirit touches you, there's no messing about, you just know it. It's not mistakable for any other feeling in the world. When God entered that car, I felt a physical presence upon me. I felt absolute joy and peace well up deep inside and come out of my mouth in a tongue that I'd never spoken before. I started giggling to myself, thinking, 'This is amazing.' When my friend came out of the chip shop he said, 'What are you so happy about?' And I said, 'You wouldn't believe me if I told you. Take me home, man.'

But then for nine days after receiving the Holy Spirit my old mates would come to my door, asking me to go out and get drunk with them. They'd say, 'I've just got my giro. Let's go out and get drunk.'

The next day someone else would turn up with a crate full of alcopops for us to drink. Every day for nine days someone would try and lead me astray with the thing I struggled with most – alcohol. And I'd go and get drunk with them.

Those nine days were horrible. On the ninth day I had a bad experience. I got into a bit of a fight with somebody and got bashed over the head.

So on the tenth day I found myself back at church. And that night I stayed at a church friend's house. After that I never looked back. I cut my old mates off from then on. I began to pray every night in tongues before I went to bed. I was reading the Bible and Christian literature. I read *Run Baby Run* by Nicky Cruz.

Then, in the summer of 2002, the church paid for me to go to Soul Survivor because they said it would do me the world of good. Soul Survivor's this massive Christian festival – I've never seen anything like it, never seen so many Christians. It was so normal to be a Christian in that environment. It was absolutely amazing.

Nicola, a church friend, paid for my train ticket down to London. It was the best summer ever. When I came back I was absolutely on fire for God.

I've grown in God so much since then. My life has changed. I don't drink or smoke now. For so many years I had a hard heart, but God has now given me such a soft heart, a compassion and love for people, especially for the lost. I don't fight now – I don't need to fight. I pray every day and I lead worship at church. I also lead a small church group.

I got married in August 2004 to Nicola, who was the very first person I ever spoke to in the church. There were lots of church people – as well as family and friends – there. It was an absolutely fantastic wedding.

My mum knew what I was like before I received Jesus and how I changed afterwards. Probably on that basis I got her and a friend along to church. They came on Alpha and gave their lives to Jesus – on the Alpha Sunday, I think.

I also led my sister, Shelley, to Christ. She's done Alpha and she's a regular churchgoer now. My brother Kieran, who's twenty-two, came from the same scene as me. He's not been in prison or been in big trouble, but he was drinking and doing drugs. He started coming to church and meeting my church friends. He gave his life to Jesus in front of a small group in our house. It was absolutely amazing.

I'd learned welding in prison, but I couldn't get a welding job when I got out. Now I work as a welder for an architectural engineering company. How Jesus brought me that job is another amazing story.

I could talk for an hour about what he's given me spiritually. And I could talk for another hour about what he's given me materially. He's given me back my dignity and self-respect; he's blessed me with a beautiful wife, a baby, a house, a car.

When I was growing up, Jesus was like a semi-fictional character. I didn't know whether he was real or not. And I didn't care. Now he means everything to me. Jesus is the Lord of my life; he's the best thing that ever happened to me. He's set me free from so much – from drink and drugs – and he's healed me inside. He's given me life in all its fullness.

Damian and his wife Nicola and their family attend a local church near their home in Bolton.

11 THE DEPORTEE
THE STORY OF DAVID JOSEPH

Born in England, David Joseph, fifty-one, moved to America when he was four. As an adult, he became a successful drug dealer, later serving nine years in prison. In February 2009 he was deported to the UK with nothing – and was left with no money or clothing at Heathrow airport. Here he tells his story.

My parents are from Grenada, West Indies, but I was born in Huddersfield because my dad had a brother who lived there and we were on holiday with him when I was born. When I was four, we moved to America because my mother had a sister who lived in New York and she sponsored us.

To start with, the six of us (my mum and dad, my sister, my two brothers and me) lived with my aunt in Brooklyn but eventually we moved out to stay in a room and we used to pay $20 a week for rent. My parents were real strict about their churchgoing and really drilled it in us big time. It was like God was not a nice person, but a God that would punish you if you did anything wrong.

My dad was a builder but at some point he started a Church of God Pentecostal church in our house. The church was our family and my cousins and their friends. There were about twenty adults and a whole bunch of kids. I spent most of my time in church or with my mum and dad – all day Sunday; Tuesday for YPE (Young People's Evangelism); Thursday for the prayer meeting and Friday for the women's meeting, which my mother used to take us to. So I was in church four days a week.

There was no going outside playing with the other kids because they were 'worldly'; we couldn't listen to the worldly music; couldn't play cards. Our only holiday was in the summer when all the Church of God churches went to a campground in upstate New York – and we had a teacher there too.

When I was thirteen, in 1972, I ran away from home and went to live with a friend of mine called Nigel, and his family. In Nigel's family, they would curse each other out and the children were allowed to smoke cigarettes in front of their mother and drink beer. I wanted freedom like that because my parents would have me so tied down. When my dad heard I had run away and gone to live with Nigel, he said, 'If you're not going to live by my rules, you have to get out,' so I never went back.

I wanted people to think that I was American. I didn't want people to know that I was a foreigner because they would tease you and call you 'boat people' even though we went to America by plane. I wanted everything that America had to offer. I used to see those big Cadillacs and pimps and hustlers – and I just wanted that lifestyle.

Nigel's brother used to sell marijuana and would use us to hold it because they wouldn't suspect kids of having marijuana. He would give us $50, which was a lot of money back then. It meant I could buy sneakers (trainers) and American clothes. I had this vision that I was going to be someone successful.

I was still going to school – I loved it – and would see my mother every day, but me and my dad could not get along because he was too religious. I said, 'I'm not stepping back inside the house,' and I didn't. But I started giving my brothers and sister money – $5, $10 at a time. They called me a hustler, which I liked.

Nigel's brother got locked up for beating up some girl, so then we started getting the marijuana on our own. This was the 1970s and the troops were starting to come home from Vietnam. They may have had half a leg or no arm, but they wanted to get stoned. Me and Nigel saw this as an opportunity to capitalise on that and we started selling marijuana like crazy. I started working my way up to a pound a week.

In Brooklyn, especially in the 1970s, there was a lot of poverty so there were a lot of abandoned buildings. We started going in the back of the abandoned buildings, knocked down the door, and we would get these kids to tell people to come to buy the marijuana so we didn't have to be on the street. That was Nigel's idea – he was real smart. We started selling about $500 a day in marijuana. I was sixteen years old, going to school still, but now I had new clothes and was able to give my brothers and sister and mother money every day.

When I graduated from high school I was able to buy a Cadillac Eldorado, brand spanking new. I had no licence, nothing. I went right up to the car lot and paid $19,000 cash.

My mum would say, 'We're praying that you will come back to church.' I'd say, 'Yeah, mum, but I ain't going to.' I just wanted to do my thing.

I met this Colombian guy named Miguel and his friend Pedro. Pedro used to have girls and I used to have girls and he'd give me girls and I'd give him girls, so he took a liking to me.

One day he asked me, 'What do you do?'

'I sell weed.'

He said, 'Man, if you want to make some real money, you need to sell coke.'

I said, 'No, man.'

I was scared of that. I didn't want to get into hardcore drugs.

He said, 'Man, listen, it can make you some real money. I'll tell you what I'll do – I'm going to give you something and you just go and give it away . . . You'll see what I'm talking about.'

So I did and I think I told one person. I didn't have to tell anybody else. People were coming up to me, 'Say, yo, you got coke too?' They all wanted cocaine. So I went back to Pedro and he said, 'See, I told you, I told you.' So I started selling cocaine. The money was coming in so much that I was scared. I had to get a gun.

Then Pedro sent me to some people he knew up in the Bronx and they said, 'We want you to move the kilos for us. We rent the cars and trucks and we pay you $5,000 a run.' Back in the eighties $5,000 a day was pretty good. So I started to move large quantities of cocaine around America – from Arizona down to Florida.

Sometimes I would get caught and I first went to jail when I was twenty-three. I was number 410191. But I never spent time in jail because I always had money, so I could just bail out and never go back to court.

I had two daughters in the 1980s – Latoya in 1982 and Keena in 1986. I was never really there for them because I was always on the streets running – but they always had everything they wanted.

Soon I was doing three or four runs a week and I was getting $5,000 for each one. Sometimes I would get a girl to ride with me and give her a couple of hundred dollars. She'd never know what I was doing. I had this chick with me one time. We were driving from Arizona to Pennsylvania and I had five kilos in the car. She didn't know and she's drinking her beer and then she says she has to go to the bathroom.

I say, 'You've got to wait till the next exit.'

'I've got to go now, I've got to go.'

So I pulled over and she disappeared up the embankment. As I was getting ready to pull off, I saw the lights in the back of the car flashing.

'Pull over.'

The police looked at me and asked me for my driver's licence. I gave them that and the next thing I knew the dog squad came with dogs and they sniffed and found five kilos in the trunk in the wheel well. They locked me up that night, put me in jail and I went to the magistrate court in the morning, which gave me $96,000 bail.

I called Pedro up. He said, 'Don't worry, where you at?' They came about four hours later and paid the money and I was out that day. From that day, they told me, 'Listen, as long as you're with us, you haven't got to worry. You just call and we'll come and get you.'

I used to keep shoeboxes of money hidden everywhere. It was hidden in people's houses and they didn't even know. I had more money than I knew what to do with. In 1994 I had another daughter, Taloya. Later I was caught in another case in New York. I was in a nightclub and somebody talked. I paid the bail, and just stayed away from New York for a while. Some years later, when I was in my late thirties, I was set up with some robbers by a girl. They took five kilos of cocaine from me and they said, 'Where you get this from?'

I said, 'Man, I'm just moving it for somebody.'

They put me in the back of a truck and said, 'If you don't tell us, we're going to kill you.' They bashed me over the head with a pistol but I wasn't talking. They took me off to some woods in Georgia and the guy said, 'If you don't tell me, I'm going to shoot you right now.'

I said, 'Man, I ain't telling you nothing. I don't know nothing, man.'

So he busted a cap in my leg with a nine millimetre. Then he said, 'I told you, man, I'm going to kill you, man.'

Then he shot me again.

I said, 'I told you, I'm just moving this for somebody. I don't even know the people.'

He shot me again in the leg. He was playing with me. It was not to kill me, just to make me talk.

Then he shot me in my stomach and wrist.

I said, 'Listen, man, I told you, I don't know these people.'

I don't know how I held on. My adrenaline was pumping. I wasn't afraid. He took the gun and put it to my head and fired it. I woke up about a week later in hospital. I didn't know where I was. I thought I was in heaven, but my mother was there. I had been in a coma for seven days.

They'd found my ID and my mother flew down from New York. My mother knew what I was doing but she didn't agree with it. She just kept praying for me. When I woke up, my leg was shattered, I had lost a kidney, I had a punctured lung. I'd nearly died. I had to stay in hospital for ninety days and had to wear a cast for three years because my whole left side was reconstructed. My mother wanted to nurse me back to health.

I had told them I was not going to go back home, but after that injury my mother said, 'Are you coming home with me?' So I started hanging out with her back in the home in Brooklyn. I even started going to church. Everybody in the church was glad to see me come in.

The question of a passport was a tough one. Because I had been born in England, I had travelled to America as a child under my mother's passport. So all I had was an alien card. My mother used to say, 'Remember, you were born in England, you don't have to stay in America . . . We'll get you a passport.' Now my mother didn't know that I was bail jumping.

'Mom, I cannot apply for no passport.'

'Why?'

'They're not going to give me one.'

She said, 'We'll try.' So she got this lawyer and I told the lawyer, 'I'm a bail jumper.'

'Well, you can get a passport, but they're going to lock you up.'

So I said, 'No, hey man, I'm not going to prison.' I knew I was facing at least twenty-five years or life in prison.

In 1998 there was the General Convention of the Pentecostal Church in Cleveland, Tennessee. My mother said, 'Why don't you come with us for the week?' And I went down there. God touched me at the convention and when I went back up to New York I don't know what happened, but I felt I wanted to get out of the game.

I drove to Pennsylvania where I had that case, you know, and I don't know what was on my mind, but I turned myself in. I called my daughter and told her, 'Listen, I'm in Pennsylvania, I'm turning myself in.'

She said, 'Are you crazy?'

I stayed in Pennsylvania for about three months before I actually got sentenced and then the judge gave me thirty-six months. They gave me thirty-six months on a $96,000 bail! I told my daughter and she said, 'No, no, they're kidding you.'

So I did thirty-six months and at the end of 2001 I was ready to go. Then they said, 'But we see here that you have a warrant for the State of New York, so New York will be coming to pick you up.' So the State of New York came and got me. I stayed there for about three months before I got to court and they gave me eighteen months on top of the thirty-six, this was about four and a half years.

Then 2004 comes and I had another case in the State of Florida. So they came and got me, and this time the judge said, 'Six years.' My heart dropped. I was crying on the phone to my mum. That was not part of the plan – not six years.

I said, 'Mom, you see what happens when you try and do the right thing?'

My mum said, 'Don't worry, God's going to work something out.'

I was going to school in prison and we had a little church on the yard. The only time I'd go to the chapel was when they had people from the outside come in.

One day in 2008 they called me up and I'm thinking, 'I'm going to get early parole. They're going to call me up to go to court.' But it was the immigration people. I'll never forget the judge's name – Rodriguez. He said, 'You're deportable.'

I said, 'How can you deport me? I've been in America over forty-five years.'

So he says, 'We see you've been here since 1963, but you are deportable because you're not an American citizen.'

They said I had ninety days to decide whether to get a lawyer and fight it. So the ninety days came up and I ain't even replied to them or nothing. Rodriguez said, 'What have you decided to do? On your release on 24 December 2008, you will not set foot on American soil again.'

I was burning mad. I threw away the Bible. I was cursing God; I couldn't even scream out, I was so mad. I began to break the rules in prison because I did not want to leave. I started messing up the count just so I could stay in America. It was so bad they locked me up in prison for forty-three days in confinement by myself.

When I got back, they put me in this cell with a Muslim guy called Raheem. I started telling him my problems. I said, 'Man, they're trying to kick me out of the country.' We stayed up that whole night talking. He said, 'Man, I heard that they've got something going on in the chapel. They're going to have food, people from the outside. They've got some kind of celebration going on.'

I went to see and they had these tables lined up with McDonalds, Burger King, Kentucky Fried Chicken, big three litres of sodas and cookies and cakes. I sat down and I ate so much it actually hurt. I had been in confinement for a long time not eating. They had this Alpha sign thing up on the prison wall. I didn't know what Alpha meant.

They said, 'OK, now we're going to have a talk,' and I guess I'd eaten so much I couldn't move. So I sat there listening to this talk about 'Is there more to life than this?'

The guy sounded more British than anything else. I didn't know what he was saying but as he spoke I just got this idea to go and talk to him. I didn't know anything about England; I had no family there; I didn't even know anything about the money.

So I went and introduced myself, and said, 'My name is David Joseph and I've got a problem. Where you from?'

He said, 'Yeah, I'm from London. My name is Paul Cowley.'

I said, 'My problem is my sentence is almost up and I'm going to be deported to England and I don't know nothing about it. Can you give me some information?'

He says, 'Do you believe in God?'

I said, 'That's not what I want to talk about. I need some information. It's critical. They're kicking me out of the country. I've got to start making some plans.'

He just kept going on with this God business. I said, 'Can you help me or not?'

Then the horn blew and it was time for me to leave but he gave me a card with the address of the church he worked for – Holy Trinity Brompton. So I went back to the cell and I just took the card and threw it in my locker. I didn't think of it until about six months later when I came across it and thought, 'You know what, it ain't going to hurt. Let me write to these people.'

So I wrote to HTB and two weeks later a big old envelope came in with the queen on the stamp. I opened it up and there were a whole lot of British newspapers sent from Paul's office. They were from a lady called Natalie. Every two weeks after that I was sent newspapers and maps and I'm reading up on it, and I'm actually feeling a lot better. They also began sending me letters and telling me all these good things.

Then on 24 December 2008 the message came, '410191, your time is up, pack up, Immigration is coming to get you.' They took me down to Miami and held me there for nearly two months. On 19 February, they tapped on the bunk: '410191, come on, we got a plane to catch.'

My mother had bought me some new clothes but they came in with a little paper gown like they wear in hospitals and some paper shoes.

'You've got to put this on,' they said.

I said, 'Where are my clothes?'

'You're getting deported, you don't wear no clothes. You're a felon. You go with nothing.'

I said, 'Not even a phone number?'

No. They searched me all over to make sure I had nothing written on my hand.

They put me in leg irons and I said, 'But ain't it cold over there?'

'Yeah, but the plane is warm.'

'But when I get there, I'll need my clothes. Will you send them on?'

'We don't know. We are Immigration. We are just told by the judge to take you there.'

They sent me wearing no clothes, just wearing a paper gown on the aeroplane, walking all shackled, handcuffed.

Next morning coming through the clouds, I could not believe I was in England. When we landed at the airport, they had just had a snowstorm.

I went through Customs and I said, 'Now what?'

One of them said, 'You've not got nobody to come and pick you up?'

I said, 'What you mean? You never even told me where I was going.'

One of the agents then felt sorry for me and said, 'You want a cup of coffee or something?' He bought me a cup of coffee and then they left.

They hadn't let me take any money. I walked around Heathrow Airport for three days in my paper gown – but I was kind of excited. It was a whole new world. I just walked around, singing all the Christian worship songs that I knew from in prison. I know Terminals 1, 2, 3 and 4 and 5. I know every part of Heathrow Airport. I didn't eat, didn't sleep, I was free after nine years, and in another world, another place, everything totally different.

All the time I was walking around Heathrow Airport, I was saying to God, 'OK, you've got me here. I was upset with you for the way you went about doing it, but I'm free. I'm going to trust you with your Word. I'm going to depend on you for everything. I'm going to trust you for my food, for money, anything. I am not going to let you go.'

After three days, the police stopped me and said, 'Are you OK?'

They took me to this room and a big, tall policeman looked at me and said, 'Would you like a cup of tea?'

He came back with this other guy and started asking me these weird questions. I found out he was evaluating me. They thought I had escaped from a mental place or something, especially the way I was dressed.

The policeman said, 'What did you do?'

I said, 'I destroyed a lot of lives – people got killed, overdosed and all this stuff. I had a hand in all that. But God has forgiven me and I'm a changed person.'

So they sent me to something called Travellers' Care where a lady said, 'I'm going to give you £10 and this map and we can send you to a place called Prisoners Abroad, and maybe they can help you.' I asked the lady, 'Have you ever heard of HTB?' and she said, 'No, I've not heard of HTB.'

I went up to Finsbury Park to this place called Prisoners Abroad and met a lady named Lorraine. I told her my story and she started crying. She said, 'I don't believe they did that.' She was a Christian lady. She said, 'Hold on, I'm going to talk to my supervisor and we'll see what we can do for you.' She came back and she said, 'We've just found this hostel. We're going to pay for it.'

They sent me down to stay in Hammersmith and each day I went back and they gave me a voucher so I could get something to eat. I walked around the Hammersmith area asking people, 'Do you know HTB?' but people looked at me like I was crazy. Prisoners Abroad really couldn't do much for me because I had no national insurance number. I was like a nobody. I wasn't really worrying about that because I knew I could make my money from drugs if necessary.

But then one day Lorraine said, 'There are some packages here from America.' They were my bundles of newspapers from HTB, which had been forwarded from the States. I pushed one bundle open. All I was looking for was the HTB newspaper and the phone number. And there it was.

I said, 'Lorraine, I need to use your phone.'

So I called up and said, 'HTB . . . hello, can I speak to Natalie?' and Natalie picks up the phone.

I say, 'Natalie, I'm David Joseph.'

She whooped and hollered.

'David Joseph, from America?'

I say, 'Yeah.'

'Where are you? We've been looking all over for you. You've been out of prison since 24 December. Where have you been?'

She gave me the address of the church office and I walked from Hammersmith Road. Natalie had told me she couldn't be there, but Kat Osborn and Jon March were there to meet me. They took me upstairs to a room and we talked and prayed, drank some coffee and prayed again.

Kat hooked me up with this lady named Jo Davies who used to call me every day asking if I was OK. She'd take me out to lunch.

I was in church the first Sunday after that – and have been ever since. I was going to all the services – all with the same sermon. By the time the seven o'clock service came around, I knew it word-for-word.

Paul Cowley was abroad when I first arrived at HTB. It wasn't until about two months later that I met him again.

I was at a service at St Paul's, Onslow Square, when I saw this guy walking past me, looking at me. 'Do I know you?' he asked. I thought he looked familiar, but when he told me his name was Paul Cowley tears came down my eyes and I gave him a big hug. I knew I had found a home in London because of him.

Sometimes I would disappear for two days and they wouldn't hear from me. Oh, man, they went ballistic. They said, 'Don't you ever, ever, ever do that again . . .' You know, genuine love, man. God really moved through them to keep me straight because reality started sinking in after about a month.

I had no money and the spiritual high was wearing off, but the church was there, especially Paul Cowley's Caring for Ex-Offenders department.

I did an Alpha course in the summer of 2009. I never stopped talking in the group discussions; I was fresh out of prison and full of Bible verses. I was in an amazing group and then I was recommended to be a helper. When I went for the helper training and saw how they do it, I had to go back to my group leaders and apologise to them for putting up with me because I was so much on fire. That was the best Alpha group that ever was, the first Alpha group, group forty-five, Tim Osborne, Tim and Jim, that group right there, and I've been doing Alpha ever since.

And I think I'm going to be doing it every time it comes around. It's a great way of meeting people, it's wonderful, it is a good thing. It's through Alpha that I'm here. If it wasn't for the Alpha team coming into that Florida prison with Paul Cowley, I wouldn't be here today. Alpha is a tool that God uses to reach people. It breaks down all kinds of walls.

I pray every day. I'm up early in the morning and I try to just walk around talking to God, for an hour and a half before my day begins.

When I first arrived in London I was staying in a hostel, but Kat and the Caring for Ex-Offenders team gave me letters to take to the housing benefit people, and I was given a one-bedroom flat – everything brand new.

I can never go back to live in America, but I can go on a visa for thirty days. I used to walk around with $3,000 or $4,000 in my pocket every day with no problem. I could do anything I wanted to do. I lived like that for years. Everything that the world has to offer – I've had it all. But it didn't make me happy.

But now I am free.

Jesus is my buddy. When you ask me what does Jesus mean to me, he's my everything.

I owe it all to him, and I thank him every minute of the day for paying my debt. I destroyed a lot of lives with what I've done and he gave his life for me. What he has done for me he will do for you. I thank Nicky and the whole team for being willing to go out and make a difference. Even if one life is saved it is worth it.

David Joseph continues to be a member of Holy Trinity Brompton, where he helps with the church's homeless projects.

12 THE SLAVE TRADER
THE STORY OF DAVE BLAKENEY

Dave Blakeney lived a violent and criminal lifestyle for many years. Here he describes how God has turned his life around.

I didn't find out until I was fifty-six that the man who brought me up wasn't my father. That was in 2006. I left school at fifteen without any qualifications and joined the army in January 1966 – a month before my sixteenth birthday. I wanted to see the world. I loved the army life – a lot of wine, women and song. I enjoyed drinking – it was part of the army culture. After seven years, I left and thought, 'I've got to find something to do.' Shortly afterwards I was driving through the centre of Manchester when I saw this guy, Pete, who had been in the army with me. I stopped, jumped out and said, 'Hi – what you doing?'

He said, 'Oh, I got a dream job.'

'What is it?'

'Security guard for a mining company.'

I said, 'Nice one – where's that?'

'Africa.'

'Wow! I've never been to Africa – been to the Far East and America, but never to Africa.'

'Do you fancy a job?'

I said, 'Yeah – I'll have some of that.'

I trusted Pete – he'd been a soldier in the same company. Then I went home and said goodbye to my family. That same day I went down to London for an interview at this mining company. At the interview the manager said, 'So, you were in the British Army? Right, you'll fly to South Africa. Then you'll get another flight from there to Angola . . .' The pay was £75 a week, which in 1973 was a lot.

I didn't know anything about Angola other than that it was a Portuguese colony, but off we went and soon after our arrival in Angola we met a policeman.

He heard we had been in the British army and he recruited us to join the government army on £250 a week. There were a few foreigners in this army. All mercenaries.

For about four weeks I hung around camp drilling the soldiers, and then one day this Belgian soldier came to me. He was called Victor [name has been changed] and had just done ten years in the French Foreign Legion. He introduced me to two other people – Pierre (French) and Curly (Dutch) and said, 'Join our gang – there's about thirty of us in all.' I said, 'Doing what?' He said, 'There's a lot of gold and diamond mines here. Well . . . we rob 'em.'

I was twenty-three and it all seemed a great adventure, so I joined and we started robbing gold and diamond mines. We also got involved in slavery – abducting tribespeople, children mostly, up to twelve years of age. We'd get an order book with a list of people. You'd take them wherever you met them – in a village or by a river. Then we'd sell them on.

I knew it was important for me not to be any different from the other guys in the gang so I had to do what they did – which included killing people. I was the procurer of the gang. I'd get anything we needed: weapons, ammunition or medical supplies.

At that time, I said a prayer to God (I had been to Sunday School, so I knew something about God). I said, 'Right, God – here's the deal. You look after me while I'm in Angola, and I promise you any Sunday that I'm in a place where there's a church, I'll go in there and I'll give it loads. I'll do whatever you want. Just look after me while I'm down here, 'cause it's getting a bit nerve-racking. Amen.'

But I managed to avoid keeping my side of the bargain. Any time I went near a township or village on a Sunday, I would always volunteer to do the perimeter patrol, so that I was outside the grounds of that town and didn't have to go to church. Meanwhile, we were making a lot of money, hiding it everywhere we could. We had four jeeps and they had solid gold and diamonds hidden under the bumpers and every other part of them.

About a year after I joined the gang, they committed an atrocity while I was away getting some supplies. They found some arms hidden in a village, which they thought the villagers were hiding for the Angolan rebel group UNITA.

So they slaughtered the entire village – about twenty people – and then burned and flattened it.

Soon after that, we got ambushed by a group from UNITA. Suddenly this massive black guy in a white shirt and shorts tried to stab me. I grabbed his hand – but my hand slipped across his knife, slicing off two of my fingers. He stabbed me again and the blade went into my stomach.

He cut like a V into my stomach. I'll never forget the look of pure pleasure in this man's eyes. I thought I was dying. Out of my peripheral vision I saw Victor. He had a shotgun with six barrels. He put the shotgun against this man's head and fired. There was this white flash and the man was dead.

Then I looked down and could see this puddle of black blood. I'd seen blood like that a thousand times before, but never on me. The puddle was getting bigger and bigger. My intestines had spilled out and I was trying to get them back in. There was no pain, but I was screaming hysterically in shock. Victor got everything back into my stomach, pulled the flap down, put a field dressing on it and tied it down. Then he arranged for me to be helicoptered out to a missionary doctor. He walked up to the doctor, took out a handgun, put it to the doctor's head and said, 'If this guy dies, Doc, you die.'

I was taken into this shack-type place and the doctor put everything back in its right place and sewed me up. I was in a lot of pain. But I was lucky that no internal organs were damaged. I guess I thought that my prayer was working – if there was a God he was looking after me. I knew I should have died.

I still wanted to carry on with the gang – we were making a lot of money.

We travelled through various countries and eventually came to Morocco. It was there that one of our gang got shot in the leg by an attacking gang on horseback. The blood was shooting all over the place. I had my hand right in his leg, looking for his artery so I could squeeze it and stop it from bleeding. But he was dead in less than a minute.

We travelled on through Spain and finally we got to Montpelier, just over the mountains, where we stopped. Pierre owned a bit of land there, so we stashed the four jeeps. He was going to sort everything and we planned to return in a couple of weeks to collect the money. So Pierre went into Amsterdam to get rid of the gold and diamonds. After about three weeks we got a call from him to go back.

I got £28,000 cash in a paper bag and went home. This was 1974 – that was a lot of money back then. I hid the money on the ferry and finally I got back home to Manchester. Then I started buying houses and renting them to students. I finished up with nine houses in the end.

In 1975, when I was twenty-five, I got married to Angela, a police inspector's daughter. She was about two years older than me. It wasn't love for me – it was convenience. I thought I'd better settle down. We had a big church wedding in Manchester. But four years later I met someone else and fell in love proper. This lady, Julie, was twelve years younger than me and was a tenant in one of my flats.

I told Angela that I was leaving her. She said, 'What about the houses and the properties?'

I said, 'You can have eight of them – I'll just take one.' I felt terrible – proper guilty. She was devastated.

I moved in with Julie and we were happy. Soon after that I got made redundant and was given £4,000 redundancy. So I said to Julie, 'Right, we can go anywhere in the world you want.' I was thinking Australia, the Caribbean, America.

Julie had never been anywhere and she said, 'Spain.' So off we went to Spain. After two days on the beach I was really bored. So I said to her, 'Let's hire a car and go and see the countryside.'

So we hired a car and drove towards Algeciras. Then I saw the ferry going to Tangiers, so I said to her, 'How would you like to go to Morocco?' So we got on a ferry and went to Morocco. I knew somebody who lived on the east side of Morocco, so we set off across the Sahara desert in a hired car. The roads were terrible and the suspension went. It was a Fiat Uno. I rang up the car rental agency and they said, 'Oh, we'll bring you another car.' I said, 'Bring me the biggest car you've got.' The next morning a big Mercedes with air-conditioning turned up. We ended up staying for the rest of our holiday in Morocco. Then we drove back to the ferry. The ferry was chock-a-block and we couldn't get the car on. So I said to Julie, 'You go over. Here's a couple of hundred quid. Get the train to Fuengirola and book into a hotel. I'll come over tomorrow morning.'

She was reluctant but I talked her into it. So I stayed there in a hotel for the night. The next day I drove the car onto the ferry. It was only a twenty-minute crossing. We reached Spain and as I was driving off the ferry, the customs guy stopped the car in front of me. Then he let the car go. So I drove forward and he waved me on. I got half-way across the ramp before it clicked that it was me they were pulling.

Then a Spanish soldier stepped out with a rifle. I thought of putting my foot down on the accelerator and speeding off – but then I stopped and thought, 'I've not done anything wrong!'

He opened the car door and pulled me out by the hair (I had long hair). Then he put dogs in the back and front of the car and they pulled sixty-eight kilos of draw out of the car. I had never touched drugs so I had nothing to do with it. I later discovered that the drugs had been put in the car before they'd delivered it to me in Morocco. The exact same thing happened to seventeen other people.

I was nicked and sentenced to ten years in Spanish jail. I then got an investigator on the case – it cost me fifteen grand in private investigators. Julie visited me every six weeks and sent me food parcels. After twelve months I got out. When I went back home I was nearly bankrupt – I had nothing.

I thought, 'What can I do? I'll go and see my mate.' He was a crook. He'd cash £50 cheques in all these bars abroad and make all this money. I started thinking, 'If I open ten bank accounts and get ten cheque books and cards, I could do that all day long and make money.' So I borrowed £1,500 and I opened a few accounts. Six months later I had the cards, cheque books and everything. And I went to France and cashed all these cheques. I finished up with £30,000 in a week. I thought, 'Well, that's not a bad income – I'll do that.'

About that time I also started on crack cocaine and heroin. And I ended the relationship with Julie. I was spending £1,000 a week on heroin and cocaine. I started smoking it, then got into injecting it. I was importing drugs from all over the world. I was also committing fraud all over the world and bringing guns to Southern Ireland (Victor was now an arms dealer). Curly had finished up as a big drugs dealer and had been shot dead.

I got married again to a Jamaican lady in about 1994. She was into cocaine. That same year I got nicked for manslaughter. I deliberately gave a drugs overdose to a paedophile who had messed with my mate's two girls. It should have been murder because it was pre-planned. I bribed people to change the statements, so it finished up as manslaughter and I got seven years in prison. I did the seven years and I've now been out seven years. That was my last sentence. When I came out of prison in 2001 I thought, 'I'm sick of this,' but I carried on with my criminal ways – importing drugs – because I was supplying the wife. She wanted cocaine at weekends, and was enjoying a life that she'd never known.

It was a life I knew I couldn't afford if I was straight. I had to make £3,000 a week turnover, without saving a penny.

We had a beautiful house in a dead posh part of Manchester. So we were living the high life and I was dealing drugs. Then one day I said to her, 'I'm sick of this life – I'm giving it up. I'm giving you a year's notice that I'm either giving up drugs or I'm gone.'

She said, 'Oh yeah – right!'

But every three months I'd write it down: 'I am leaving in nine months, unless we do something about this drug habit and the way I'm living.'

When the year was up at the beginning of 2002 I said to her, 'I'm going for a paper – see you later.' And then I left. She hadn't worked out that the year was up – even though I'd given her a warning every three months. I walked out and took just £4. I left my cars. I thought, like an idiot, that I'd just come off the drugs.

I then lived rough in town, in different places. I might sleep at the station one night if it was raining. I made myself homeless – I'd had enough of the way I was living.

I'd worked for all these gangs – dealing them drugs – but I just wanted to get out of all that. I had this idea that I'd go to Birmingham or Leeds or Montpelier. But I didn't – I just lived on the streets.

No one knew where I'd gone, and nobody spotted me on the streets. My wife had no idea where I was. I'd left everything at home – including £30,000 stashed all over the house. I left my wife everything.

One evening I went to get a sandwich from a guy who gave out sandwiches and brews to the homeless from a converted ambulance. His name was Steve.

That evening he said to me, 'Why don't you go on Alpha?' I said, 'I don't want to go on Alpha – what's Alpha?' He said, 'If you've got any questions about God or anything, you can ask.' I said, 'I haven't got any questions.'

I knew there were a lot of God-botherers about in town. Another day he said to me, 'Come on Alpha.' So I said, 'Tell me again what happens on Alpha.'

So he said, 'It's on Wednesday night.'

I said, 'Well, that's out.' On Wednesdays I used to go to my mate's house to watch Coronation Street. It was getting really exciting at the time. He said, 'I'll pick you up at seven o'clock here in town. You'll get something to eat.'

'Ah – you never mentioned that before. Something to eat?'

'Yeah.'

'But it's on Wednesday . . .' Then I thought, 'Hmm . . . we get something to eat. That's Wednesday covered.' I'd only eat once a day so I said, 'Yeah – I'll come with you.' I only agreed to go because of the food. It was held at a place called SMCF – South Manchester Christian Fellowship. Steve took me the following Wednesday.

There were about twenty people there, men and women, all homeless. Steve brought them all in his bus. After the meal a speaker gave a talk – different people spoke each week. But the talks went right over my head. I still had a drug habit – I was smoking heroin and cocaine. I'd injected until I'd used all my veins, so I had to stop injecting. I couldn't stop taking the drugs – I wasn't as strong as I thought I was. Throughout that course I read the Bible so that I could ask a question that they couldn't answer – but they always had an answer. Then we had a Holy Spirit day in the church, but nothing happened to me. All I was interested in was getting my food covered for that day.

Then Steve invited me to another Alpha a few months later. I was still on drugs. Again, I went for the meal. Then he said, 'Do you fancy going to church on Sunday? We'll go for something to eat afterwards.' So I thought, 'Something to eat – Sunday covered.' So I said, 'Yeah, I'll go to church.' We went and it was a baptism service. Everybody was so friendly and the place was rocking. As I looked around at everyone I thought, 'Wow, I wonder what these people have got . . .' I could see something in people's faces that you don't normally see. They had something. So I said to Steve, 'I wouldn't mind a bit of what they've got.'

Steve said, 'Easy one that – ask Jesus into your life and you'll get it.'

I said, 'No. Someone dying for me 2,000 years ago? I don't think so, mate. I can't even get my wife to make me a brew – and you're telling me some geezer's died for me?'

He said, 'Do you believe in God?'

I said, 'Of course I believe in God. Common sense tells you everything has got to be made. So yeah, I believe in God.'

'Then ask God for understanding.'

'All right. I'll pray every night when I go to sleep.'

He didn't know I was still on drugs. Just before the second course had started I'd been injecting again. I'd been off injecting for about a year, and some veins had come back. So I started praying every night. I had conversations with God – but nothing fancy. I said, 'Here you are, God. Give us understanding about your lad, because I can't see it at all. If you give me understanding I'll be buzzing. Thanks. Amen.' But before I prayed I'd have an injection, because it's easier to pray or do anything when you've had a dig.

The next night I'd say, 'Here you are, God. Give us understanding about your lad – 'cause I can't see it. Amen.' And the next night and so on. This went on for four months. I'd completed a second Alpha course by then.

Then I prayed, after my dig, 'Here you are, God, I'm getting proper fed up now. This has been going on for four months. I've been praying and asking you about your lad. And there's just no way . . . So please, get it sorted. Amen.'

The next morning I woke up and understood perfectly why JC died for me. Perfectly. I was buzzing to the max. That was in 2003 – I was fifty-three. And I couldn't wait until that night to tell Steve. I had to wait all day – until 9.00 p.m. – and it was killing me. That night I said to him, 'I'm buzzing – I can see it! I understand why JC died for me. I'm buzzing to the max.' And he was so pleased. He said, 'Are you coming to church tomorrow?' And I said yes.

The next day we get to church and three-quarters of the way through the service I'm thinking, 'Hang on, I've been a smackhead for twenty-odd years. But I've not had a dig since Friday . . . I should be writhing in pure agony all over the floor. I should be sick, I should have diarrhoea, all my bones and joints should be shattered.' But I felt fine. I haven't touched drugs since. I'd been through the withdrawal symptoms before, when I'd been in prison, so I knew what to expect. But I had no symptoms at all.

So that was it – I gave my life to Jesus that Sunday. I said a prayer: 'Jesus, I want you in my life. I'm really sorry for all the mess that I've made of my own life. Come into it and straighten me up. Amen.' My life changed dramatically after that. I wasn't a smackhead any more. I was living in a hostel by then – but within a week I was offered a fantastic flat – a one-bedroom council flat.

Then I got a part-time job. I hadn't had a straight job since 1982 – more than twenty years before.

I got Hepatitis B from the drugs. It stays in you for years. The hospital said it would be a twelve-month course of injections in the stomach and that might not sort it.

For five months I was at it – loads of people praying for me. Five months later it had gone. So just five months of prayer and injections and the hepatitis was gone. I got baptised on Easter Sunday 2003. I wish I could have been a Christian from a young age – brought up as a Christian, in a Christian family. What a life that would be.

I drive the homeless bus now, to pick up all the homeless people to take them to Alpha. I speak to them about going on Alpha and I say to them, 'You get a free meal – that's your day covered.'

Now I pray every day and I read the Bible every morning at 5.30. I go to church. I had one guy – Danny – come to my house to do Alpha at midnight one time. He was a smack-head and the smackheads can't come on Alpha at 7.00 p.m. because they're busy scoring then. One night he was desperate to score some drugs. So I prayed for him. I said, 'Here you are, God. I don't want Danny to score. Danny doesn't really want to score. And God, you definitely don't want Danny to score. So get it sorted. Amen.'

So then I said, 'Right Danny – you pray.' So then he said, 'Well, Dave's right, God. He don't want me to score, I don't want to score and you definitely don't want me to score. So like he said, get it sorted. Amen.'

I was stood there looking at him, going, 'Danny, are you all right?' I could see it in his face – I knew exactly what was happening to him. I was thinking, 'Nice one, God.' The peace was coming right over him. It was amazing. He hasn't touched drugs since and is now a Christian.

Every choice that I've ever made has been my choice. I don't blame it on my parents or friends – every wrong turn I ever made is down to me. I know that I've been forgiven for all my past.

There's a sign in church about human trafficking – and I hate that sign because when I see it, I see slavery, and it always brings back my past and what I did. I would say to anyone who's not a Christian: Get JC in your life – it's the best move you'll ever make. He's your provider, your best mate. He's alive.

Dave Blakeney attends a local church in Manchester. He and his friend Danny continue to help at a local home-less project.

13 THE ANGRY MAN
THE STORY OF BRIAN ARBLASTER

Brian Arblaster was 'angry about everything', and would lash out at everyone around him. Brought up in a spiritualist home in England, he emigrated to Canada, from where he tells the story of how his life has changed.

I was born and raised in Brownhills in what was then Staffordshire (now the West Midlands) and I have three sisters. My family, including my mother, father, grandparents, uncles and aunts, were all involved in spiritualism. My mother was a medium and would consult the dead in small spiritualist churches. My mother constantly told me that 'the spirits were watching over me' and she was 'contacting the spirits on my behalf', but I would kind of patronise her and just say, 'Yeah, OK Mum,' and sort of leave it at that. I only ever went once when I was eighteen and I thought it was a complete sham.

They had a meeting once a week on Sundays and they would sometimes invite itinerant mediums to come and do their reading. They would give them messages from dead people in their family. My mother never really brought it to the home; she would always go to someone else's home. She never did it in front of us because I think my sisters and I were pretty cynical about it, pretty removed from it. What it did do was start to make me interested in the occult and I studied it a lot from around thirteen or fourteen years old.

I loved horror movies and was a huge fan of Edgar Allan Poe, probably America's greatest horror story writer, and a fellow called H. P. Lovecraft who created a whole world of 'older gods' as he called them, which I found fascinating.

But the occult scared me and I thought, 'If I get involved in this, it is going to cause me problems.' I only ever tried the Ouija board once or maybe twice and frankly I got nothing from it. It didn't work for me. I think possibly it was because of my cynical attitude. I was open to learning about it and the study of it, but what I found scared me enough to keep me away from it. My father wasn't really much of a participant in this – he was more a member of the congregation – but my mother was very interested.

My mother was kind of cool, never very emotional, never very loving. My father was probably closer to us than my mother. I don't ever remember my mother hugging me, I don't ever remember her telling me she loved me and my father was too embarrassed to say it.

As I got to about fifteen years old I started hanging out in pubs. There was a pub around the corner from where we lived which would allow younger people. I got a girl pregnant when I was eighteen and so I had to get married. It was traumatic. I'd probably been going out with her about six months and she got pregnant.

Basically my father said, 'You made your bed; lie in it. You're marrying her,' so I did. My first daughter, Julie, was born just about six months after we got married.

I was eighteen and cocky – and had no idea how to run a marriage, no idea how to bring up a child. I knew nothing. I was a party boy and I would drink to the point of numbness. I used to do it pretty much every Friday and Saturday night.

Then we had another daughter called Jane. I tried to be the best I could but after about ten years I'd had enough.

Stupidly I had an affair and lived with the lady for about two years, but it was a terrible relationship. It was based on sex. Can you imagine? I mean, how shallow . . .

My wife Dorothy was wrecked, absolutely wrecked. She was just beside herself, a mess. I started to have an affair with a colleague's wife, Heather, and she left him and married me. That would have been in 1985. We lived together for a very short time, maybe six months, and then we married and moved to Canada. A long-term friend of mine had come to Canada thirteen years earlier and started his own business in tool and dye, and he said 'Come out,' so I did. I thought, 'I've pretty much wrecked England. I may as well go over there and wreck Canada now.'

Before I left England my eldest daughter Julie started seeing a black man and I just flipped out. I was incredibly racist; I hated black people and I said, 'If you're going to do this, this is it. You will make a choice right now – him or me – because I will not be your father if you're going to marry a black man.' She started to cry and there was a lot of yelling and swearing from me and she just sat there crying. It was a terrible thing to do. I said, 'From this point forward do not contact me, do not call me "dad". I don't want no more to do with you.' I walked out and Heather was sitting in the car outside and she said, 'What's going on? I could hear you yelling,' and I said, 'I don't want to talk about it.' Eventually I told her and she said, 'Well, maybe you should rethink this. She is your daughter,' and I said 'You shut up and mind your own business.' Then my youngest daughter took the side of my eldest daughter (obviously because that was right), so I didn't have any contact with them for about ten years. Julie eventually married the man, whose name was Paul. My new wife was never fully convinced that the move to Canada was the right thing to do, but I was.

I was still drinking on Friday and Saturday nights. On Fridays, it was the boys – a bunch of loud, drunken, obnoxious guys like me – and on Saturdays it was another crowd. I liked girls – I'm a guy, right? – and I couldn't control it. If it came across my path I was going to participate. I had no self-control; I didn't want any. I was running my life. I hated the church. I had no interest in it because it was so boring and it was so controlling and it wanted to take over your life and say, 'You can't do that any more.' I thought, 'There's no way I'm going to get involved in anything like that.'

My mother died before I came out to Canada, probably about 1983. I never felt that close to her, to be honest. We never had that mother-son bond thing going on. She had a heart attack. My dad was about 58 when he died. That was the first time I can remember crying as a man. That was traumatic. My father was a good man and he didn't deserve me. He was a very moral man actually and he had a son with no morals whatsoever, not really. I was part of this post-modern movement that said, 'You know what? I can do what I like, when I like. No one has the right to tell me what to do. I am the author of my own destiny. I can pretty much control my life.' And my father was not of that background. I'm sure he was disappointed by me.

He never said that, because he was too good a man to say that. I deeply, deeply regret that I never told him I loved him, never. It's not a word we used in our family.

I eventually made up with my daughter Julie. It was at a family reunion and I walked over to her and said, 'How are you doing?' and she said 'Good,' and she started to cry and I put my arms round her and said, 'I'm sorry, I've never stopped loving you,' and it was true. But I was too pig-headed and stupid to listen to my own heart. I lost ten years for nothing, because of my own obstinacy, pig-headedness and racist rubbish.

Meanwhile, Heather and I were two damaged people in a marriage. We partied together and we had people over and we'd do all of the stupid things that people do to hide the fact that they are who they are. We'd go out and party all night and there were times where we would skinny dip with other couples and stuff like that in their swimming pool. We did all kinds of really ridiculous things, drink all day and through into the night until we virtually just fell down. We lasted seventeen years.

I have worked for the same company for twenty-two years and they're a great company to work for. There is a

Christian group in this company and I used to love ragging these guys. There was one in particular who I hated with a passion. I hated the sight of him; I hated his presence. He would walk into the tool room where I was working looking for something and I would just rail on him and curse at him, call him names, give him such a hard time. He never retaliated. I could never understand that and it used to make me more angry at him. His name was John Riosa and he was a born-again Christian. Then there was an Irish guy called Dominic who was a Catholic born-again Christian and I didn't like him either. Well, he's Irish, I'm English, and I would call him 'Bomb chucker' and say, 'How can you blow up women and kids and call yourself a man of God?' He'd walk away and I hated that. The thing I hated most about Christians was that they wouldn't fight back. I thought they were just a bunch of hypocrites that got together on Sunday morning to praise the Lord and then go out and do what they like all Sunday afternoon.

I was angry about everything – politics, football, religion, people. I was very bitter, very angry. There was a lot of resentment, even though I'd got everything I possibly could have had. I had all the material things. On my 50th birthday I went to the Rock and Roll Hall of Fame in Cleveland and when I was coming home I thought, 'I've got a wife, I've got a house, I've got cars, I've got a truck, I've got a good job, I've got all the things that the North American lifestyle is supposed to give you to bring you peace and happiness and yet I don't have that peace and happiness . . . There's still this piece of me missing, like I'm not fulfilled. What's the problem?'

Finally I went to work one day and I was talking with Dominic (the Irish Christian) and later he said, 'Are you OK?' and I said, 'Yes, I'm OK, why?' and he said to me, 'You talked to me for fifteen minutes and you didn't swear once.' I said, 'Really?' and he said, 'No. What's going on?' I said, 'You know what? I don't know. Good talking to you,' and I walked away. He said to me, 'You know, maybe you should come to church.' I replied, 'Out of the question, no. I'm not ready for this.' And he said, 'Well, come to church on Saturday night. It's a nice gentle evening, there's no pressure to do anything. Just come and have a look.'

He kept at me for a couple of weeks so eventually I went to church. When I got there, I found it was a gentle church and some people were obviously emotionally moved and there were tears and I was thinking, 'This is nuts.' But I went along the following week . . . and the next. Then Heather started to come with me. Every Saturday night I said, 'You know, I'm done, I'm not going back,' and then about Wednesday I'd think, 'Well, I'll just give it one more try.' But I didn't participate. I just sat at the back of the church.

Then they started to run their very first Alpha course. At church one night Dominic came up to me and said, 'There's this course, this Alpha course and it's for new Christians and people who don't know Christianity all that well. You should go. You have all of these questions, you have all of these difficulties with the faith, why don't you go on the course?' At first I said no but then I realised it was an opportunity for me to step forward and to say, 'You people are deluded, you are walking in complete darkness, you don't know this is complete rubbish. You are being completely manipulated and I'm going to tell you that right.'

I went to the first one on a Monday night, without Heather. There were maybe thirty people and the food was actually not bad, I was quite surprised. We had dinner and then we watched a DVD of Nicky Gumbel. I was fascinated by the video. I found Nicky kind of amusing, because he was a fellow Brit. At the group time, I said, 'I certainly don't believe in God and I have no idea why I'm here,' but I went back the next week. Then Nicky started to talk about the 60,000 documents that they have and the Dead Sea scrolls and the validity of who Jesus was. He talked about Josephus and Pliny the Younger and I thought, 'Right, I'm going to scribble these things down and I'm going back home to check on the internet.' I did that and thought, 'Oh.'

Then on about the fourth week they began referring to Bible passages. They said, 'Turn to John' or whatever. I had nothing to say because I was late finding the passage so I wasn't very participative. The following week Ray, one of the co-leaders, called me to one side and said, 'You've always given us your opinion but last week all of a sudden you stopped doing that. Why?' I explained about not finding the passage, at which he said, 'Ahh, you sit by me and I won't start until you have the place.' I thought 'He's kidding.' Nobody had ever been that nice to me. I was not used to being treated that way. I thought, 'Wow, that is so cool.'

Then came the Holy Spirit weekend and we went away on this retreat, which was great. But nothing particularly happened to me until the drive home. Then, as I was driving along I said to God, 'OK, God, if you are there (and I think you are) I'm going to ask you to come into my life. I want to see what you've got, so do what you like. Carry on.' That was as close as I'd ever come to praying, but, boy, did he ever come into my life and show me what everything was. He came into my life so much.

All of a sudden, it's like I had this sensitivity that wasn't there before. Things smelled differently. Everything tasted better. I thought, 'There's something going on here,' so I went to Dominic and said, 'I've said this prayer thing, and things are changing and what am I supposed to do?' He said, 'Well, you can pray and ask the Father to help you,' and I said, 'OK, right.' I had no idea what that meant.

At the end of the Alpha course I thought, 'I don't want to lose this amazing camaraderie that we've built within the group,' so I did the follow-up course on Philippians. Then I asked if I could take Alpha again and they said, 'No, but we can have you in as a helper if you like.' So for the next course I was a facilitator. I would pass the tissues to those that wept and make sure that the food was in the right place and all of that. I sat in on a group and occasionally I'd throw in a comment or two.

In the meantime I'd been practising this prayer thing. But then came a big shock. Six weeks after I prayed that first prayer, I found out that Heather was having an affair with a colleague at work. That came as really quite a blow. I got roaring drunk and got on my knees in tears and said, 'You are supposed to be this God. I'm trying to come to you and this is what I get to show for it. This is it.' I was very angry. Heather and I tried to make some kind of sense of it all and struggle through but eventually I said to her, 'I'm done with this. This is just not working.' So she said, 'Well, I'm going back to England.' We divorced and she went back to England and I stayed on in the house that we bought together. I blame myself, I really do. If you nurture your marriage, if you love your wife and you take care of her she is not going to look at anyone else, so I don't blame her for what she did. It's my fault. I've taken responsibility.

I started to pray more and then someone said to me, 'You know, I think you have a gift for this prayer thing.' Then they invited me to join the prayer ministry and so I pray for people – particularly those in pain. When someone is hurting I have this instant 'Oh let me pray for you' thing.

After the divorce, there was a group of us that used to go out for coffee after church on Saturday night. One of the girls was called Donna and I thought she was kind of cute. I asked her out but she said no and I thought, 'OK.'

Some time later, I prayed, 'You know what, Lord? I need to have a lady in my life, so please bring her along.' Not long afterwards I invited Donna out to tea and she said yes. A year later, in 2003, we were married. She is amazing. She's got a heart as big as Texas; she is a wonderful, gentle, sweet, beautiful Christian lady.

I'm still in touch with my daughters and they have noticed a difference in me. I never told them I loved them before Christ, but now I tell them over the phone all the time. I talk to Julie's husband now and he's a great guy. I get along great with him. We go out and have a pint, stuff like that. I wouldn't have done that before Christ. I originally made up with Julie before becoming a Christian, and shook hands with Paul then, but I'm closer to him now since becoming a Christian. I have one granddaughter, Jane and Des's daughter, Chloe.

When I look at my life the way it was, and I look at what Christ did for me on that cross, I am baffled to understand that he would think someone like me was worth it and it just brings me to tears. I never could understand why women wept at weddings. I know now why: it's all about joy. I now attend church regularly . . . You'd have to beat me to keep me out of it! I'm there every Saturday night and then Donna and I go on Sunday morning. I read my Bible and pray on a daily basis, all day. I have found that not only is he the God that created the universe, he's God of the little tiny things too and so you can ask for stuff that is amazing.

If someone had asked me about Jesus fifteen years ago, I would have said, 'He was a conman and started his own religion for whatever reason and the rest of you are totally delusional because you've fallen into this trap of self-delusion by believing in this non-existent God.' Now I think he's sitting here with us right at this moment listening to every word. I don't know where I'd be without him. I dread every second of not being around him. To have him in your life changes everything. It changes your perspective, it changes your feelings.

He took away all of the garbage from my life, forgave me for all of the things that I've done, and allowed me to live. I don't have words to say how grateful I am.

Brian Arblaster and his wife Donna continue to attend church near their home in Ontario, Canada.

14 THE SCAFFOLDER
THE STORY OF GARY FLYNN

Gary Flynn made such a success of his scaffolding business that by 2008 he had moved into a £1 million house. But within a few weeks his life was ripped apart when he was diagnosed with cancer, he lost his home and his business collapsed. This is his story.

My dad was a scaffolder, same as me. But I don't remember him too well. When I was six or seven years old, he was putting up scaffolding at a house in Deepcut in Surrey when he was killed. My uncle and he were working together and my uncle said, 'Come on, Jimmy, let's go to breakfast.' My dad, who was quite a conscientious worker, said, 'I'll just fill this last bit in and then we'll go.' At that, my uncle heard a boom, boom, boom. He looked round and my dad had fallen off the scaffold. It turned out that a stray army bullet from the firing range in the army barracks had hit a tree, ricocheted off and hit my dad in the heart.

I was at school when it happened. My headmaster came and took me out of my classroom. He said, 'Your dad's had an accident and he's been killed,' and he took me home in his car. I remember walking into the room in my grand-mother's house. I can still remember the wallpaper, the furnishings. I went in and my mum was lying on the sofa crying her eyes out. There were lots of family there. The curtains were drawn.

They didn't think it would be good for me to go to the funeral so I was taken into the town centre but the bus route to the town centre went past the cemetery, so I actually saw the burial from the bus. It was a very big funeral. Dad was a popu-lar man. Mum got compensation after a while. The army said it was an accident and gave her . . . I think it was around eight-een grand, which I suppose was a lot of money at the time.

Over the years I've met scaffolders who knew him. They've said things like, 'I remember your dad. Oh, he was a lovely bloke.' He was a really good person, full of life.

When my dad died, my mum's way of handling her grief was to push me away. We moved in with her mum and dad and my grandparents really brought me up.

My nan was my best friend. Granddad tried to take my dad's place and was very strict – but my nan always defended me. She would say, 'He's gone through enough.'

I went to secondary school at Richard Aldworth in Basingstoke. I was good at school, played for the school football team, a bit of rugby, a bit of basketball, a bit of table tennis. I was good at drawing as well.

When I was fifteen my mum got remarried to a pilot in the American army. He had been in Vietnam and flew Cobras with the missiles on the side. When they got married, he was stationed in Germany and then they moved back to his home in Texas. Mum asked me to come but I didn't go at first. Later I went but didn't enjoy it and came back. I wasn't really happy in either place. I'd been drinking from about the age of fourteen. Me and my mate Dave would go down to a pub called the Buckskin. We were quite big lads. I'd save my money all week and go to the Buckskin on a Sunday evening – disco night – and get tanked up.

Then I got married at eighteen to a girl from school who I'd known for two or three years. In the space of one year I got married, had a baby son, Tony, and got divorced. We broke up because I got caught with two other ladies. I was messing around, yeah.

I overdosed after that. I was back living with my grand-parents, aged about nineteen. I got drunk, came back from the pub and just thought, 'You know what – I hate my life, I hate everything. I found loads of tablets that my nan and my granddad had, filled a pint glass up with them and drank them down with water, and left a note. I remember waking and being slapped around the face. 'Wake up, wake up!' There was my grandfather in his underpants and my uncle, who was staying that night, and my nan. They brought me round and I was rushed to hospital and had my stomach pumped.

After that I tried America again for a bit. In the end I came back and got back together with my ex-wife, and we had another son, Joe. By then we were living in Hammersmith. We didn't bother remarrying. We used to take turns looking after the baby at night.

One morning when Joe was nine weeks and six days old, it was my ex-wife's turn. She was asleep on the sofa, the baby was in the crib next to her. I walked in, crept past the crib to put some tea and biscuits down, and then crept back out. A couple of minutes later I heard a scream and I ran into the room. She was screaming, 'The baby, the baby's dead!'

Joe was still in his crib. I pulled him out and he was dead. I screamed, 'Just phone an ambulance!' I tried to revive him but he was well gone. He was a cot death.

Four or five years later we had a third son, Jimmy, and he slept in our bed with us for four or five years, with a monitor, because we were so worried about having a cot death again.

I think I only stayed with my ex-wife because of the children. When I was twenty-nine I started having mental health issues. I started having panic attacks on the tube and I thought I was going to die. I would get pins and needles and kept thinking I was having a heart attack. I went to A&E loads of times – so much so that they would say, 'Oh, here he is again. Gary – there's nothing the matter with you.'

We lived in a penthouse in Bayswater at the time and I told my ex-wife to lock the balcony doors and hide the keys because my mind was telling me to jump off the penthouse and kill myself. I was put on some medication but gradually weaned myself off it over the next two years. I was just training my brain to say, 'Listen, you're not having a heart attack.'

My ex-wife and I were not getting on well. She told me time and again that she had had enough of my behaviour. One night I went out with my mates and we had a row when I got home. I thought, 'You know what, I'm going . . .' and I left; I left her everything. Something clicked in my mind. I had started up a scaffold company in Fulham with two friends and I moved into my Portakabin, which was my office, in my yard.

A year or two later I bought myself a house in Worcester Park and my eldest son Tony came and lived with me. He was fourteen or fifteen at that time. It was a three-bedroom house and we had no furniture to start with. I just had a kettle, some knives and forks, a couple of plates, and some blow-up beds. We had quite a big front room and me and the boys used to play football in there. Gradually I bought some furniture.

Two years later Tony moved back with his mum. When he was eighteen he told me he was gay. He was very frightened when he told me. He was shaking. I said, 'Why can't you just tell me what's on your mind?' Then I actually said, 'Are you gay?' and he sort of looked down and went 'Yeah.' I put my arm round him, gave him a cuddle, and said, 'Listen, you're my son.'

When I was thirty-seven, my nan died. She had been suffering from emphysema and I visited her in hospital. She said, 'Oh, I really fancy a bacon sandwich,' and we sent someone to the hotel down the road to get her a bacon sandwich. I lay next to her in her hospital bed and held her hand and said, 'It's all right, Nan.'

I drove back to London and later that evening I got a phone call, saying, 'Nan's gone.' I suppose she was in her late seventies, early eighties – not that old.

That was a really bad time. Throughout all my times of trouble, she had been my stability, so losing her was a massive, massive thing for me. I would go out on these huge drug and drink nights, ending up in the houses of people I didn't even know. I was drinking probably in excess of twenty pints, if not more. When you're having cocaine, it suppresses your mind and you just keep going.

My second cousin Joanne came to my nan's funeral and we would speak every day after that. They say one door shuts, another one opens . . . It's weird. Joanne says she had fancied me when I was a child even though she was younger than me. She lived in Liverpool but within six months she had moved down to live with me. She's seen me through all of that darkness. When she moved in I was still crying a hell of a lot and I'd go out, take cocaine, alcohol, whatever.

Anybody else would have said, 'What am I doing? I've just left my whole family in Liverpool, I've come down here and you're doing this to me. I'm off.' But not Joanne. She stood by me and slowly took me out of that.

She is a wonderful, stable person who was good for me in every way. She stood by me no matter what, through thick and thin, when things were good, when things were bad. That's rare to find. We've talked about marriage many times but have never got round to it. We kept putting it off, saying, 'Maybe next year.'

Meanwhile, my business got really, really successful and it came to the point where I could buy a house in West

Chiltington, West Sussex, costing the best part of £1 million. It was one of those things that you've always dreamed of. It was a massive house with a swimming pool, hot tub, gym in the garage, land . . .

By December 2007 I'd exchanged contracts on the house and completion date wasn't till the following July, but we had money coming in and there was no problem. I exchanged on 5 per cent of the price of the house and we agreed that we would move in on the exchange and pay nearly £1,000 a week rent until completion in July.

One day in June – some months after Joanne and I had moved in – my grandfather came over and we sat in the garden having a drink, looking over the pool and the lights and the hot tub and everything else. As we sat there, he said, 'Son, I'm really proud of you. No one's ever given you nothing and you've had a pretty hard life, but you've got on with it and built a successful business and now you've got all this. You must be really happy.'

There was a slight pause and I heard myself saying, 'Happy? No. I hate my life, I hate me, I hate everything about it apart from Joanne, and my children. I hate where I'm going. I've got no direction. What's going to come after this house? A two-million-pound house? A five-million-pound house? Ten-million-pound house? Where's it end? I don't know what I'm doing – fancy cars, nights out. I just hate it.'

The words came out of nowhere. I knew I wasn't happy, but at that moment with my grandfather it really came out. I had probably been working and travelling for eighteen hours a day at that point because the business was starting to struggle. I had also been feeling a bit unwell. I was having persistent tummy trouble and went to the doctor. I was sent to the hospital where I had loads of tests, cameras and this, that and the other. I was asked to come in the following Monday for the result of a scan.

I went in and was ushered into a room with two doctors. They said, 'I'm sorry, Gary. This time it is cancer.' It hit me like a bus and I hardly know what happened next. I just ripped my clothes off, took my jewellery off, got down on my knees and said, 'Doctor, don't let me die, please don't let me die, I don't want to die.' He said, 'No, listen. It's bowel cancer and if it's diagnosed early there is lots we can do.'

I left the hospital and got into the car. Joanne drove. I phoned my son Tony, who was working for me at the time. I told him to meet me at his brother's house. I said, 'I need to speak to you both.'

He said, 'OK, Dad. What's the matter?'

I said, 'Just go to the house and I'll see you both there.'

So I got to the house where they were waiting. My ex was there (Jimmy lived at her home with her) and so was Joanne, of course. I told them to sit down and I said, 'I need to tell you something.' I told them and my younger son went, 'Dad, you ain't going to die, are you?' I'll never, ever forget that.

I said, 'Son, I can't tell you that. That's not in my hands . . . but you know what? I don't want to leave you and I'll do everything I can so that I stay here with you.'

Then I just broke down. I had to walk out. Joanne and I went to Sainsbury's where I bought the largest bottle of

Jamaican Spice rum, a bottle of lemonade, a bag of ice and a plastic glass and I sat in the car park in Sainsbury's and drank the bottle of Jamaican Spice Rum. I was quite numb for the whole next day. I told the people that worked for me, who were all shocked.

The next day I woke up and said out loud to the sky, 'Right, you're not taking me from Joanne and the children.' And I decided to fight then.

Who was I saying that to? I don't know. It was just in my mind. I'd never been to church apart from weddings and funerals.

There was just one strange thing that had happened some seven years before. I was putting up some scaffolding and this young lad wearing a hoody came up to me. I thought he was coming over to borrow some money for some drugs or alcohol, but he said to me, 'Do you know about God?' All the blokes on the scaffold with me were telling him to get stuffed and get out. I went, 'Oi, leave him alone.' He stood and spoke to me for about ten minutes. A couple of weeks later I sat in my office and thought, 'I'd like to see that lad again.'

And then a bizarre thing happened. The fellow walked straight into my office there and then. I didn't know him, didn't know where he lived . . . It turned out he had recognised the company name on the signboard outside and walked in. I went, 'You know what, that is amazing. I just thought of you . . .'

He said, 'Shall we go and buy a Bible?'

I said, 'Yeah, come on then,' and in the middle of my business day we drove to Hounslow Trinity Church and bought a Good News Bible. I never saw him again. I read the Bible a couple of times but then just put it in a shelf at home.

From the moment I was told I had cancer, my business life began to fall apart. Because of my illness, the mortgage I was due to have on the new house was pulled and I lost every penny of the 5 per cent deposit. I had also bought £28,000 worth of furniture and I lost all that. Within a week, Joanne and I had to move out of the house into a caravan in my yard in Hampton Court.

I began to wonder if God had heard me scream, 'I hate my life,' because a week later, I had the cancer, the mortgage pulled, and boom, in a caravan. My business also went into freefall and I had to lay off all my staff except for one.

When I was diagnosed with the cancer I was nearly twenty-one stone. I was told keyhole surgery might not be a goer because of the size of me.

The operation was booked for two weeks later.

I said goodbye to everybody because I was sure I was going to die. I didn't say, 'I'm going to die' to everybody because I didn't want my kids to think that, but inside I did. I told Joanne and my mum and stepdad, who flew over from America.

When I said goodbye to the boys, I gave them a kiss and cuddle and said, 'Just remember your dad loves you.' It was horrible.

Just before I went into the theatre, Joanne said to me, 'See you when you wake up,' and I went, 'I ain't going to wake up.'

She went, 'Yes, you are.'

Six hours later, I woke up in an intensive care unit with a cable from my neck, and I had all this stuff on my chest. When my mum saw me, she said, 'You look the best you've looked in years.' Very soon I said, 'I feel all right' and I started asking for food and drink. The doctor said, 'Give him a cup of tea.' The next day I was eating and on a ward with everyone else. They were quite shocked how quickly I recovered. By the fifth day I was allowed home to the caravan – in fact it was a brand new caravan by now which my mum and stepdad gave me as a present.

Then the chemotherapy began. It meant going to Charing Cross on a Friday all day. They would feed me chemotherapy through my Hickman lines and then send me home with an American bum bag and inside was a plastic bottle and inside the plastic bottle was a balloon, and inside that was the chemo.

Over the weekend, that balloon would shrink, feeding the chemo through this pipe into my neck for three days, and then Sunday night, you have to disconnect.

Just before the chemo started, Geoffrey, a friend of mine who is a fruit and veg stallholder in Fulham, came to see me.

He went, 'Alrighty, how are you doing, mate?'

We sat at my caravan, outside in the sunshine, and he went, 'So do you reckon you're going to kick the bucket or what?'

And I went, 'I hope not, God willing.'

He went, 'God willing? Do you believe in God?'

I went, 'I don't know. I hope there's something there because I need some help. I'm looking at maybe dying.'

Two days later, the phone rings. Big deep voice. 'Hello, Gary, it's Geoffrey. I'll pick you up in the morning. We're going to Alpha.'

I went, 'What?'

He said, 'Just be ready.' He said it was something to do with the church.

You don't say no to Geoffrey, so next morning he picked me up and took me to this church in London called HTB. As we walked in, we were met by these two ladies – Pippa and Helena – and Geoffrey said, 'This is Gary, he's got cancer . . .'

So I sat down and everyone was so lovely and friendly. I never felt out of place. I really enjoyed the first week and I even went to church the following Sunday. It was the 11.00 a.m. service at St Paul's in Onslow Square and when I went in I thought, 'This ain't a church. This is all right.' There were bacon sandwiches, coffee, sofas, cushions, lots of young people there. It was such a lovely welcoming feeling.

I began to look forward to Alpha. Everybody I met in the church were blinding, absolutely blinding, wonderful, friendly people. They made me feel as welcome as in my own house.

Then we had the Alpha weekend, which was held in Chichester at a holiday centre. I was given my own room because of the chemo and I just loved it. On the Sunday morning, there was a chance to welcome the Holy Spirit into your life.

I thought, 'I'll stand at the back by the door.' I had heard about this speaking in tongues business and I just thought, 'No, I don't fancy none of that.'

When they said, 'Come, Holy Spirit,' I was out the door, bang. I got really angry walking back to my room. I was swearing at myself saying, 'You idiot, you're never going to get right. You're going to end up down the same road as you always did.' When I got back to my room I lay on my bed and cried violently.

And all of a sudden, I felt a presence in the room and I thought, 'Wow, what's going on?'

While I was in my Alpha class, someone had come in with little bookmarkers with Holman Hunt's picture *Light of the World*, showing Jesus waiting at the door. There's no handle on the outside, and it was explained that you have to open the door and welcome him in. So when I felt this presence in the room, I said, 'If you're there, Lord, come into my life. Please, Lord, I need you. I need saving.'

It was like I was floating, I just felt this mass presence of peace, of love. I was crying and I went, 'Just save me, I don't want to be Gary no more.' I'd had enough of Gary.

'I hate me, I don't like me, Lord.'

After about thirty minutes, a couple of people came to the door and said, 'Are you all right, Gary?'

I said, 'Something's happened.'

Later, one of the leaders, Michael Emmett, sat down with me and said, 'Tell the Lord your sins and don't hold anything back.' And he prayed for me and said, 'Come, Holy Spirit. Gary's here, your son.'

When I went home, I felt completely different. I felt this peace. I told Joanne the amazing thing that had happened.

A few weeks later, before the Alpha course had finished, I was staying at my grandparents' house in Basingstoke.

Lying in bed I sat bolt upright – eyes wide open – in the middle of the night. A beam of light was coming from the ceiling into my tummy and moving round. I sat looking at this light coming out of the ceiling into my tummy. It was like someone was pushing a hand on to my tummy and moving it around.

Then I looked to the right of my bed and Jesus Christ was stood there with his hands out. I just said: 'Thank you, Lord, oh thank you, Lord.' I lay down and closed my eyes. I left it for a couple of minutes and opened my eyes again. He was still there.

I wasn't scared and I just thought, 'Well, you've come to me, Gary the scaffolder. You've come to me.' I knew I didn't deserve it.

From that day on, I can't get enough of Jesus. He has taken over my life. That was November 2008.

I was carried by God all through the chemotherapy. The two times I felt sick during a Sunday service I went, 'God, you know how much it means to me being in the church. I don't want to walk out of the church if I'm feeling really sick.'

And it was like someone pressing a switch. In that instant my sickness just went. That happened on two occasions.

I often think of Psalm 40, which I used to read when I started my chemotherapy.

'I waited patiently for the Lord's help; then he listened to me and heard my cry. He pulled me out of a dangerous pit, out of the deadly quicksand. He set me safely on a rock and made me secure. He taught me to sing a new song, a song of praise to our God' (GNB).

I used to swear a lot – all day, every day. Now my swearing's stopped . . . well, by 95 per cent. When I stopped, people began to say, 'What's happened to you? You've got a peace about you. What's happened?' And I'd say, 'I'll tell you what's happened: God. I found him and he found me.'

When I heard that HTB was sending a team to Brighton to plant a church, I offered to put up the scaffolding around the church. Now it's up and we have some banners advertising the Alpha course on it. Since then I've put Alpha banners on every scaffolding that I put up, so it's putting the word out there. Even if it's up for a day or two, someone's going to see it, someone's going to go, 'Oh look at that, I wonder what that means?' and hopefully they'll have what I've got.

Since Alpha, our group still meets every other Thursday to do Bible study, which is fantastic. Not every person turns up, but most people come every time and Geoffrey's obviously still there.

I pray every day and I have my Bible with me all the time – the same Good News one I got years ago. I'm also reading *The Message* version by Eugene Peterson.

When I used to go out, I used to binge drink – I'd drink until I dropped. I don't do that now. I've never looked at a line of cocaine in over two years now. I don't miss it. I've been in a situation where all the boys were out one night and an old acquaintance came over, 'Here you are, Gary, a gram of coke; help yourself.' And I went, 'I don't do it no more.'

I had been really frightened of going out that evening because I knew that there'd be old people from the past. But I didn't get drunk, I didn't take cocaine, I didn't end up with no women, I didn't wake up in some strange house . . . I got home at a sensible hour instead of an ungodly hour and I woke up in the morning fresh as I went out, with no hangover. That's a massive thing for me. That's a miracle, definitely, without a doubt.

Joanne has seen the difference. One day I think she will come on Alpha but in her own time.

You know what? Jesus is my dad now. I think of him as my dad.

Just a short while ago, I was staying at a hotel for a birthday party. I woke up in the morning without a hangover, had breakfast with everybody, and while people were sitting there having tea and coffee and toast, I went into the garden, in the sunshine, sat on a bench, and opened my Bible . . . As I read my Bible, I closed my eyes and felt Jesus sat next to me on the bench – next to me as though I'm sitting out in the park with my dad.

Now when I pray to the Lord, I am able to say, 'Lord, if you want, take my business away.' For me, that's a big thing to say.

I now go and help out once a week at the evening homeless shelter in St. Stephen's, Twickenham.

Over Christmas 2009, the Lord provided us with our first flat. We had been in the caravan for the best part of a year and half.

I feel, since I found God, my life's just begun. Forget the last forty years, it's just begun now. It's a fresh start. I've got God in my life and I know he'll be there when I die.

There's lots of people that have hurt me really badly and I've tried to make my peace with them. I've called them or

I've bumped into them and said, 'Listen, I've had an amazing experience. I've found God in my life and I don't want to fall out with you or be your enemy.' And that's it.

If I praise the Lord, I cry. It's like a block of ice being hit with a blowtorch and I just melt. I melt in his presence, it's just absolutely amazing. I'm a completely changed man and I don't ever want to go back to my old self. God came at the perfect, perfect time.

Gary Flynn continues to be involved both at Holy Trinity Brompton and his local church in Twickenham.

15 THE INMATE
THE STORY OF MICHAEL EMMETT

In November 1993, Michael Emmett was caught by police masterminding a massive importation of cannabis into the UK. He was sentenced to twelve years in prison. While in prison, he became a Christian and began a long battle to sort out a life which had become complicated in many different ways. Here he tells his story.

I was born in Stockwell, south-east London. My dad was part of the criminal scene in London. He knew Ronnie and Reggie Kray; the 'Great Train Robbers'; the Richardsons; and many of the famous personalities who were around at the time. He was a boxer and had a bit of a reputation. It wasn't an easy life.

He owned drinking clubs in London as well as two night clubs in Doncaster and Nottingham. But I don't know where he got the money to start them up. Maybe he stole it. He bought cars, he sold cars, and held illegal gambling games.

In 1965, when I was seven, he decided he didn't want this life for his family any more and he moved us out to New Malden in Surrey.

My mum was a typical south London woman. She wore her hair bouffant-style, with false nails, false eyelashes, and high-heeled shoes.

We looked totally out of place in New Malden, but to me my mother was always an angel.

One day, when I was about nine, I got home from school and my dad had gone. I asked, 'Where's my dad?' and was told he was away working in the army. But I kicked up a great fuss. I was tearful every night and in the end they decided it would be a good thing if I saw him.

They took me to Brixton prison and I can remember walking in. My dad was sitting behind a glass partition and I wasn't allowed to touch him.

He had been charged with armed robbery and was on remand. It had a profound effect on me. I was never allowed to tell my friends that my dad was in prison because he was trying to better us as a family.

This is when the lie began. Never being able to speak the truth went hand in hand with a criminal lifestyle.

Some months later, my mum said to me, 'Would you do me a favour, Michael? Would you go upstairs and turn the bath off? I've left it running.'

I walked into the bathroom and my dad was standing there. I couldn't believe it. He was like my idol. I just thought, 'My dad's home!'

He didn't serve a jail sentence that time – but he did serve a couple later on in his life.

At school, I did quite well until I was about fourteen or fifteen when I disconnected. I was a bit of a rebel by then and couldn't wait to have a cigarette and a beer and to kiss a girl. I flunked all my exams.

At sixteen I left school – I just left – and my dad said to my mum, 'I'd better take him with me.' He was running a car hire business at the time.

When I was twenty, I branched off on my own and started buying and selling antique furniture with a friend of mine in Chelsea. It was all under the counter.

In 1981 I got arrested for handling stolen property. We had picked up a beautiful mirror from a building in South Kensington. A lady saw us leave and gave the police a description of the van.

They found me and I got put on remand in Brixton – the place where I'd been to see my dad some fifteen years earlier. When I got there, I found I knew people in the prison. I was no Al Capone, but in my fraternity people know each other. That was my first taste of prison. I was twenty-three. I was later fined and given a suspended sentence.

I had started taking drugs cocaine and cannabis when I was about nineteen or twenty. It was the in thing. But cocaine transforms one's personality. You dance with the devil, and there ain't two ways about that.

I was an addict and I started selling drugs to support my habit. I was going through five or six hundred pounds' worth a week sometimes.

Around that time I met a girl called Tracy and we got a flat in Colliers Wood. In 1983, she became pregnant and our daughter Aimee was born.

Then, one day later that year, I came out of my shop in Battersea with another bloke and got into his car. The police knew I was a rascal and they followed us and we had a police chase. I didn't want to stop because we had cocaine in the car.

My mate was driving and I was in the back. After about four or five miles we tried to drive through this fence – a corrugated fence. But behind it were some concrete pillars and we smashed into one of them doing about forty or fifty miles an hour.

This other guy went through the windscreen and was badly hurt. It was pretty horrible. I broke my ankle and dislocated my knee. As I lay there in pain, I remember an old lady coming up and hitting me with her walking stick. I think we had just driven through her garden.

I remember lying there saying, 'Listen love, I really am sorry. Please, I'm in an awful lot of pain here' as she was whacking me across the body with a stick.

We got arrested and were put in hospital prison. I had internal bleeding in my ankle.

I was fortunate to get bail. A friend of mine's mother put her house up for me which meant that I could stay out of prison for a year before the case came up.

Then I got a message that we were going to court in four or five weeks, so I went round to my friend's mother and said, 'Go into the police station and withdraw the bail.' She withdrew the bail – and I immediately got on a plane to Spain on a false passport. I went to Marbella. That was 1985.

Some months after that, my brother Martin came out to see me and one night we were taking cocaine together. He wasn't a drug user, but he tried a little bit.

After that, we had a real bad argument about my father splitting from my mother. We started arguing and he walked off at four in the morning to go to Malaga airport.

I ran to him and said, 'You can't go . . . but if you must, take the car.' On the way, he drove under a lorry and died. I just couldn't believe that happened.

He left a message written in Vaseline on the mirror in my bathroom, saying, 'I love you'. I've still got it today. His girl-friend was three months pregnant at the time.

I didn't know anything about it until the next day when I started phoning England to speak to Martin. It wasn't until that evening that I found out. I rang Ted, my brother's friend, and said, 'Is he back there yet?' Silence. I said, 'He's dead, isn't he?' And Ted said, 'Yeah'. The Spanish authorities had contacted the family in England.

I couldn't believe it. I just couldn't believe it. And I went to see him in the morgue. They had covered him up as best they could. It was absolutely horrendous to see him. I bent forward and kissed him – and he still had his sweat on his forehead.

That was the moment I lost the plot and became emotionally disabled. I blamed God and used to scream at the church, 'What have you done to my brother?'

We put him in a beautiful coffin of Spanish oak and we flew him home. I had to come back because of the funeral. That was in August 1985.

My mum and dad were going through a rocky patch at the time and when Martin died, it nearly killed my dad. He was wrecked with shame and guilt. The whole fraternity of people around us suffered when Martin died. It was like an atomic bomb had gone off.

That was when my mum and dad separated. I was still wanted by the police, but I managed to keep out of their way for a while. During that time, Tracy fell pregnant and our second daughter Lillie was born the following year. But by then I was in prison.

I had gone to Harrods to buy some clothes in the sale and I had an argument in the car park with a guy there – a stupid argument – and he phoned the police. When they came, they worked out who I was and that was it.

When I went to court, I was looking at about five years, but I had a great defence and I got a 'not-guilty' on the main charges and I only got sentenced to eighteen months on a misdemeanour charge. I was out after ten months.

When I came out, I was determined to marry Tracy and live an honest life, but I started taking drugs again.

My third daughter Beth was born in 1988. Things then became very unmanageable because my life was steeped in drugs. I was doing £1,000 a week, taking drugs – mostly cocaine – on the hour every day if I could.

I also used to drink a lot. I loved champagne.

I've never been a violent man, but I've had a lot of anger and got involved with very volatile relationships. My nickname is The Bear, but my bark has always been worse than my bite.

I could see my whole family were broken-hearted about me. I was a mixture of opposites. I had everything in my life which was good, and I had everything which was bad. I was full of fear, yet I was fearless. I was very happy, I was very sad. There was no middle ground. The scales were always at one end or the other.

Tracy and the girls went to live in Epsom while I was living in Sutton.

At that time on my own I then hit rock bottom. I had no money, I was behind on my mortgage, and I was emotionally on the floor. I was going to the pub every day, drinking. Soon after that, Tracy went to see her mother in Hong Kong with the children.

One afternoon at about 4.00 p.m., I was sitting in the house smoking cocaine when the drug squad knocked the door down and flew into the house.

They obviously thought that there was a big stash of cocaine there but there wasn't. It was just my personal stash which was quite significant.

Tracy arrived back from Hong Kong later that day to find me handcuffed to the bannister in the loft conversion with about twenty policemen there. And they took me off to the police station.

When I went to court I got a drug counsellor who was huge in the field at that time to come with me to say that I was a drug addict and that I needed help.

The court ordered me to attend something called the Promise Unit – a drug recovery programme – but it didn't work.

Tracy and I weren't getting on so in 1991 I decided to go and live back in Spain. When I went, I left a trail of destruction behind me caused by my drug-taking, my womanising, and my criminal life. I had a bad reputation.

In Spain I got involved in selling crisps to bars. That was all straight but in the meantime I was camouflaging something else. I started getting involved with importing drugs. I was looking for the quick buck – the big buck.

I was involved with an importation of four and a half tons of cannabis on a boat to a place in the West Country. It had a street value of about £9 million.

We put the cannabis into yellow fish-boxes. We put the cannabis in first, put the ice on top of that, and then put the fish on top of that.

I flew in from Spain to meet the boat. I hadn't meant to go because as an organiser you should keep away – but I just wanted to make sure it worked. What I didn't know was that the others had already all been nicked by the police.

So as we drove into the village at 11.45 at night where we were due to meet the others – with one guy driving me and a friend in the back – suddenly there was this big halogen light shining at us and thirty police officers – ten of them armed – surrounding us. They shouted out on this big megaphone, 'Get out of the car and put your hands on your heads.' I couldn't believe it.

I was in the passenger seat and I shouted to the driver to accelerate, but he just collapsed saying, 'I'm not doing that . . .'

He was quite right as it was a very dangerous situation and it was a crazy thing for me to say. They came for me and my feet didn't touch the ground. They just spun me round, lay me on the road and handcuffed me.

As I lay there looking at the stars, someone said to me, 'A penny for your thoughts.' I just said, 'My three children.'

All my phones had been tapped, all my cars were bugged – both in Spain and in England.

I'd been aware of something but I'd chosen to dismiss it. I thought I was more clever than they were. Anyway, they took me to Exeter jail and when I walked in I thought my life had finished. That was November 7, 1993.

My dad, who was helping me out, got arrested in a hotel in Brighton. They were watching him and after arresting him they brought him down to me. So we both ended up in Exeter prison and were put in the same cell.

When they took us to court from the prison, we were taken in a van with the sirens going and police cars and a helicopter overhead. There were armed officers all around us because of the seriousness of the crime.

In the end, I got sentenced to twelve and a half years, and so did my dad. Twelve others were sentenced as well, including a fisherman, some boat people and a fishmonger.

In prison, I had something of a tough guy image but what no one knew was that I was breaking up inside. For the first few months in prison, I was using cocaine and one day in my cell I got 'the Fear'. I got really frightened. It was horrendous.

Anyway, there was a Bible in the cell with an index in the front which pointed you to bits of the Bible related to stress. I just picked it up and started to read some of these passages. Then, as I read, for one split second I thought, 'Hold on, I feel all right.'

And that little mustard seed was all it took. I thought, 'Wow, I want that. That is what I need if I want to be well.'

That was 29 June 1994 – and after that I started going to chapel.

Once, we had a South African preacher visit and there was a time at the end when you could follow him in a prayer giving your life to God. I said it out loud and asked God to forgive me my sins. My dad was sitting next to me.

It was then I went on a Christian course they called Alpha. I liked it and after that, although there was still the old Michael there, I started to change. I stopped the drugs, the smoking and even the swearing. I was very rigid about it.

I had a lot of ridicule about it all because of who I was. Other people in the prison thought I was just working my ticket to get parole.

Soon after that, I got involved in some charity work in the prison. A friend of mine at the time knew Samantha Fox [the former topless model and singer] and we decided to invite her to come down, which she agreed to do.

She came to the chapel which was situated on the wing in the prison so I was able to get her out on to the prison landing. The lads couldn't believe it.

Anyway, I got talking to her about the church. I'd read about her going to a church called Holy Trinity Brompton and I asked her about it.

She started talking about this guy called Nicky Gumbel and I said, 'Who is this Nicky Gumbel?'

She said, 'Well, he's the guy that runs this Alpha course they do at the church.'

When she'd gone, I said to Bill Birdwood, the prison chaplain, 'Why don't we ask Nicky Gumbel to come down, Bill?'

He went, 'Oh no, no I can't . . .'

We were in his office and I said, 'Come on'. So he got the number and phoned Nicky Gumbel.

We got through to him and I spoke to him. I said, 'Well can't you bring a team down?' He said, 'Look, I can't come myself, but I'll send a team down.'

And a team from Holy Trinity Brompton came to the prison in November of '94.

The person leading it was someone called Emmy Wilson and I loved the godliness in her as soon as I saw her.

About twenty or thirty of us attended the sessions. At one point Emmy taught us a song called 'Jesus I love you deep down in my heart' which was really good and got everyone rocking.

Anyway, at the end of the session, they prayed for the Holy Spirit to come. And this guy Lee Duckett started praying for my dad. Suddenly my dad started laughing – and I'd never seen anything like it. It was like a transfiguration. It was like he was 30 years younger. His face was completely changed. He was laughing so much that the prison authorities accused him of drinking. He said, 'There's only one Spirit I'm on and that's the Holy Spirit.'

Everyone else was joining in too by now and I wasn't sure what was going on. But I was sure it was God. I saw healing going on in my father. I saw his face.

Soon after that – in March 1995 – we were moved to Swaleside Prison in London. It wasn't an easy time because our reputations had come before us and everyone knew we were coming. Then suddenly we turned up as Christians.

People went, 'What are they doing going to church? Are they weak?'

I detected some people were a bit offish but I just got

more loud and boisterous and pretended to be one of the chaps.

On the first Sunday, Dad and I went to chapel and it was absolutely dead with maybe five people.

So while in Exeter we had been kind of protected by the love of Jesus, with about thirty or forty going to the chapel, this was a working prison in London and it was different – harder – where 'everything goes' if you understand me. But God looked after me.

The chaplain was a guy called Roger Green who was a lovely man with lots of enthusiasm.

We told him about Emmy and got him to call her up from his office and we started an Alpha course in the prison. We got loads of people to come to it – around one hundred guys, many off my wing. It was wall-to-wall in the room where we did it.

But it was very hard for me because I had to walk there past all the other guys and they knew where I was going. They didn't make it easy. It was a nightmare. But at the same time I enjoyed it – and a lot of people changed. The course had a profound effect on their lives and real seeds were sown.

After that we moved on to Maidstone. It was a good thing to be moving prisons because if your behaviour improves, they lessen the category of your prison.

In Maidstone I started to slip in my spiritual walk. Things were changing in me. There was a lot of stuff coming out of me that God was dealing with – a lot of anger. While in Maidstone, Dad and I went to the appeal courts and we got three and a half years off our sentences.

I believe that was the work of God without a doubt. So that meant we were now eligible for parole in a year and a half's time.

We were then moved to an open prison in Kent called Blantyre House. There, the church was just diabolical. I still used to go to church every Sunday morning, but I'd wear my football kit as I played in goal for the prison team immediately afterwards. I was getting over the embarrassment of going to church by then.

Every nick [prison] Dad and I went to, we got a Bible study together where we used to pray. We used to make sure we met at night and we'd have a pray at about quarter to eight of an evening. That happened in most jails that we were in, which was encouraging. It was good.

While in Blantyre, we arranged for Emmy to come down with a team. They set up an Alpha course, but the course only got started after we had been moved.

Our next move was to Latchmere open prison in Richmond, where you go to work. The church there was OK, but Sunday was an open day with your family and when you came back off your town visit, you'd go straight to church, which wasn't ideal.

When I had my parole interview, the parole officer (who was a retired barrister) was looking through all my bits of paraphernalia. Suddenly she said, 'Oh you've done Alpha.'

So I said, 'Before we go on, I don't want you to think that I'm holier than thou, that I've become born again and I'm going to save the world. I believe in Jesus, I'm a Christian, but I'm not planning to use that as a way out of jail.'

She said to me, 'Oh no, I just wondered . . . Where did you do Alpha?'

So I said, 'I done it in Swaleside and in Exeter.'

She went, 'Where does Alpha derive from?'

I said, 'From Holy Trinity Brompton.'

She said, '[HTB Vicar] Sandy Millar's a friend of mine.'

Well, I couldn't believe it. I just thought, 'Thank God. That's unbelievable.'

I came out of prison in 1998.

In the meantime, Tracy and I had had a reconciliation. Towards the end she started to visit me. (My children had visited me throughout my prison sentence and I remained very close to them.) When I came out of prison, I had all good intentions but I started drinking – and then one day I used cocaine again. I started using drugs only for a little while – once a week for about three months – but I'd run to the Bible stoned, get on my hands and knees and think, 'What am I doing?'

Emmy said to me, 'Michael, be careful of the devil's schemes.'

I decided one day I'd had enough. The conviction in me wouldn't allow me to go down that road again. I went and saw Emmy and then went to Narcotics Anonymous. I haven't had a drink – or taken drugs – since.

Why did I pick the drugs up again? I believe the reason I did it was because I was pent up and locked away for a number of years – and after that a prisoner is vulnerable. Then if you're not in a good church and surrounded by the right people, you're going to slip. You're definitely, definitely going to slip. But I did come out into a good church at Holy Trinity Brompton. Even then, it takes time to tidy up twenty-two years of carnage, because that's what it was.

Tracy and I have not had an easy time since I came out of prison. She did the Alpha course and developed a relationship with the Lord from that course. But life together wasn't easy. The insanity in me wanted to be very self-destructive and wild. We were always the best of friends through everything – through failed relationships, through prison, through my drug addiction . . . She is an angel. But when I came out of prison, she wasn't ready and obviously I wasn't.

In prison, you don't have any responsibilities other than turning the light on and off and presenting yourself where you are told to go – like the gym, work, food, visits.

When I came home I could sense there was a change in me because I didn't want to be involved in crime. I didn't want to hang out with the boys that I knew. Aimee, Lilly, Beth and Tracy had a good union and I used to run around on the periphery having single relationships with all of them. I was committed to my kids. I think that God did deal with me in those days – and there was a lot that God had to do.

I continued going to church and chatting to Emmy and the others – and going on prison visits with Alpha. I also helped with lots of Alpha courses at Holy Trinity. But my relationship with the Lord is a continuous fight. I now have a relationship with God that is deeper. Trust was a big thing for me in life and now I've had my own experience of trusting God. There are times when I know that he is not very happy with me but it doesn't mean to say that he doesn't love me or that my world is going to end.

When I'm not doing what God wants me to do (and I'm not talking about crime here or anything bad like that – l'm talking about attitudes), I really sense God saying, 'Sorry, l'm not in that. That's not where we're going. This is where we're going.'

There is a scripture in Haggai which reads, 'Give careful thought to your ways. You have planted much, but have harvested little. You eat, but never have enough. You drink, but never have your fill. You put on clothes, but are not warm. You earn wages, only to put them in a purse with holes in it' (Haggai 1:5–6).

Basically, God is saying, 'You're busy doing your own thing. Do what I want you to do and I'll make that a lot better'. I sense that there is a big calling on my life, not necessarily to save the world, maybe just to save me and my family. That would be good enough. I'm now learning about humility.

I used to like cars – it sort of went with the territory – but now I'm realising that they are just lumps of metal. They don't have a lot of meaning for me any more.

Being a Christian is tough.

In the world that I live in I have to be a warrior. It might sound mad to anybody else but it is a fight for me and those voices are strong. I was on drugs for seventeen years and my brain was insane, but God is now restoring me. I think Narcotics Anonymous and Alcoholics Anonymous are great and people find their sanity through them. But for me, without shouting from a soap box, the love of Christ is the ultimate. The important thing for me is not to get too religious with the traditional rules and regulations but to accept the love of Christ Jesus into my heart and allow him to make the changes.

My message to anybody struggling with the struggles I had is to hang on, believe in the Lord, do Alpha – in the nick, in church, or wherever. It's about keeping it simple.

The girls can see that I've changed. They know that it is Jesus who has done this. The Lord is still working on me. I read the Bible a lot now. It's a source of life for me. I pray now too. I prayed before becoming a Christian but they were just selfish prayers – prayers in times of desperation. Now I love praying. That's my forte – it's my bread and butter. I pray in the car – everywhere, at any time. Jesus has made such a difference in my life.

Michael Emmett remains a member of Holy Trinity Brompton. He continues to visit prisons and speaks at Alpha courses there. He has seven grandchildren. He says, 'God has never let me down.'

16 THE ATLANTIC ROWER
THE STORY OF MARK STUBBS

In August 2004, fireman Mark Stubbs was attempting to beat the record for rowing across the Atlantic in his boat Pink Lady *when the boat was hit by a hurricane 300 miles off Cornwall. Just before the hurricane struck, he made an unusual vow. Here he tells the story.*

I was brought up by the sea and was one of those children always drawn to physical challenges – always looking for the next tree to climb. As a schoolboy, my main interests were rugby and boxing.

I left school at sixteen and joined the Royal Marines after seeing the colour brochure with its emphasis on training and adventure. But a month after my eighteenth birthday I was sent to the Falklands. I was one of the youngest there.

I don't like to talk about it – it was one of those experiences where you no longer have control over your own life.

I certainly didn't believe in what I was fighting for. The Falklands were an awful long way from England and I felt like a bit of a pawn in a big political game. But there wasn't much time to question because you had to focus on surviving.

I lost a friend down there. I could easily have been killed too. After that I wanted to get out. During my time in the Falklands I did question where God was. I felt so far from God when we were being blessed on board the ship before going to fight – I didn't think that God had anything to do with war.

Paula and I had been childhood sweethearts – going out with each other since we were eleven. We split up for a bit when I first joined the Marines but then, when I was sailing to the Falklands, I sent her a letter saying how I really felt and asking if we could get back together. From that point we started corresponding again.

I left the Marines eighteen months after our return from the Falklands – after doing five years. One of the last things I did with the Marines was to be part of their fifteen-man team working with Richard Branson on his Power Boat Challenge attempt to break the Atlantic speed record. It failed 100 miles off Bishop's Rock when the boat hit a container and was holed.

I married Paula dressed in uniform just before leaving the Marines – a traditional family wedding. I felt very far from God and didn't feel that he had anything to do with my life, but I wanted to marry in church.

I joined the fire service in 1985 and have worked there ever since. To save someone's life is a fantastic feeling

– what other job can offer you that? I work with a team of ten guys. The great thing about the fire service is that the shift systems allow me to spend time with my family as well as providing lots of time for other activities.

I started canoeing in my early twenties when I was looking for a challenge. I did the Devizes–Westminster Canoe Race – a 125-mile race from Devizes in Wiltshire to London's Westminster steps – eight times. I have also done about eight marathons including the London Marathon. I always seem to be in need of a challenge.

Our two daughters, Brianna and Victoria, were born in 1991 and 1994.

One day in 1995 I was at work at the fire station when I saw a newspaper on the table. It was *The Times* and one particular headline caught my eye: 'Ocean Challenge to Rival Everest'. It was an article about how Chay Blyth [former record-breaking Atlantic rower and sailor] was organising a race across the Atlantic from Tenerife to Barbados – 2,700 miles. All the two-man boats were going to be identical and you had to build your boat yourselves. The race had never been done before.

I read the article again and again – and then tore the page out of the paper. I kept mulling it over and it burned a big hole in my pocket until I took it out and pinned it on the board in our kitchen. Paula and I had long talks, but eventually she supported me in doing it.

We had to raise £40,000 from sponsors but eventually I did the race with a friend from work – Steve Isaacs. It needed two years of preparation and was hugely pressurising.

It took us fifty-eight days and we finished in sixth position. We set off on 10 October 1997 from Tenerife and reached Barbados on 8 December. Those fifty-eight days at sea were the first time in my life where I was completely away from the outside world. We had no communications with anybody – no phone or anything.

A few months after our return, I started planning my next challenge, which was to row across the North Atlantic from St John's, Canada to Britain in a record-breaking time. It took four years to organise the four-man team and the boat was called the *Skandia Atlantic Spirit*. We set off from St John's in 2002 with BBC cameras on board filming a documentary.

But twenty-one days into the trip – when we were exactly halfway across – we hit a bad storm, a force ten, and it ripped our stainless steel rudders' fittings off. We managed to replace them but the boiling seas snapped them again. That was the end. There was nothing we could do but wait. It was fifteen hours before a passing ship rescued us. It was desperately disappointing and, once back at home, I started planning to do it again.

Meanwhile, for some time Paula had felt that something in her life was missing. Her best friend had become a Christian two years before on an Alpha course and suggested she did the Alpha course herself. One day, she timidly mentioned to me that she would like to do the course. Did I mind? I didn't have any problem with it at all. I didn't not believe, but I had enough challenges – what more did I want?

So Paula went on the course. She was very quiet about it and I didn't ask her much. Once the course ended she started going to church. She enjoyed it and looked forward to going. I was surprised. For me church was about being preached at and being told that you're a sinner.

My girls went to church as well – and they got as much out of it as Paula did. I saw a real change in them and it stimulated some interest and discussion in the family. I saw my daughters become closer friends by becoming Christians. I went to church with them a couple of times but just sat on the sidelines. I thought they were lovely people there.

Meanwhile I was working towards my next trip in 2004. I advertised for new crew and got new sponsors – same route, same idea. We made over fifty improvements to the boat and changed the rudder system completely so that the boat itself would break before the rudder . . .

This time the crew was a former SAS man called Pete Bray, a guy called John Wills and a *Times* journalist called Jonathan Gornall. Our boat was called *Pink Lady*.

In August 2004, we set off from St John's once again and encountered tough weather early on. The Grand Banks are notorious – that is where the Titanic went down – and there were 1,400 icebergs around us and it got down to minus ten.

Each of us was rowing for two hours on, two hours off. While two slept in a watertight area, the other two rowed on the open deck – which was a bit like sitting on a surfboard. When it got rough, you got wet.

After thirty-eight days at sea, we'd travelled 1,800 miles and were thirteen days up on the record. There were just 300 miles to the finishing line in Cornwall.

For some days our support team back in England had been monitoring the progress of a hurricane called

Hurricane Alex, which had been moving up the east coast of America. Often these hurricanes move across to the Azores where they are broken up by the high pressure – but this one set off across the Atlantic and seemed to be travelling in our direction.

At that stage, we were hit by a storm, which got to force ten – with fifty-five mph winds – and gave us the roughest night I'd ever spent at sea. It was scary to think that it might only be the beginning.

On 7 August, we were told the hurricane was twenty-four hours away and I sat everyone down and went through a complete safety brief for three hours. By the end, we were as ready as we possibly could be.

There was no question of pulling out. For a start, we had all committed ourselves to finishing the race before setting out. Secondly, you need to give the rescue team three or four days' notice if you are going to give up. No, we were going to see it through.

For the last twenty-four hours before the hurricane hit, we had force seven to eight winds and a clear blue sky. We were surfing down these fantastic, rolling waves and it was the best rowing throughout the whole trip. The boat was performing really well. Then Lee, our weather router in America, phoned us on our satellite phone to tell us that the hurricane was expected to reach us at about seven o'clock. We finished rowing and I made a phone call to Paula back home.

That was a really surreal situation. Paula was back at our home in Poole on a lovely warm summer's day with not a breath of wind. I could hear Victoria and Brianna out in the garden playing – they were having a barbecue. Paula had heard that bad weather was coming our way but I said to her, 'Don't worry about it . . . I think our boat will stand anything.' I spoke to each of the girls in turn and tried to sound cheerful, not wanting to panic them. Then I had to say goodbye and it was a really horrible, gut-wrenching feeling.

I put the phone down and immediately thought, 'I don't feel I said goodbye properly to Paula . . .' – so I called her a second time and had another chat, which was really nice. Then I said goodbye again. After that, I sat strapped to the deck, with the sea anchor out, and started thinking about my life. I knew I was at a point where I could die and I thought to myself, 'I have a beautiful family, my life is full of adventure, but is there more to life than this?' I realised there was something missing deep down in my heart.

I thought, 'Perhaps I should go on an Alpha course.' I'd seen how it had affected my family, how they'd changed. As I'd kissed Victoria, my younger child, goodbye in her bed before I left, she had said, 'Look, Daddy, if you get into a situation where you feel that you are going to die, I'd like you to say a prayer asking Jesus into your life.' She was very concerned that I wasn't a Christian. That memory went through my mind while I waited for the hurricane.

The black clouds were on their way – I could see them. The sea was getting more and more violent. At that point I made a promise to God that I would go on an Alpha course if I got home. I said silently: 'God, if I get back alive, I will go on an Alpha course and find out more about you and the peace and love you've given my family.'

The hurricane came incredibly quickly – it took just two hours. One moment it was blue skies on the horizon, the next it was completely black all around and it was so noisy you couldn't hear. The roar of wind, rain and waves was just phenomenal. There were 100 mph winds ripping down the side of the boat. The rain was incredibly hard – you couldn't look into it. The noise of the rain even drowned out the wind.

To start with, I sat completely upright on the deck (the others were in the two little cabins – one at each end of the boat – so I was alone) – twelve inches above the water – and decided that instead of being scared about the situation, I would get the camera out and start filming.

Each wave was like fifty feet of sheer tooth of water. For a few seconds, it was like being on the top of Mount Everest. The next minute I couldn't see anything because the boat was completely covered with sea spray – then up we would go again. It was like the sea was just erupting.

The sea turned really black at that stage and it became too dangerous to sit out any longer. We each had to wedge ourselves into these little cabins – I was with Pete in the front one – and hold on tight. If you relaxed in any way your head was bashed around and cut.

All I wanted it to do was stop. There was no conversation with anybody. You couldn't concentrate on anything except for the next wave – and they were getting bigger and bigger. Each wave made the boat pick up speed, and fall down the face of the wave. That lasted for five very long hours.

Then, at 1.30 a.m. on the morning of 8 August, we rose up a particularly big wave. It sounded different and we braced ourselves as the boat picked up speed and turned upside down as it fell.

Then there was an explosion of noise as the tiny boat was broken in half by the full force of Hurricane Alex. Within seconds, Pete was on top of me and water was pouring into the cabin.

We were upside down and we had to get out. That was a scary time. We had to let the water fill the cabin, take a deep breath, open the cabin door and swim under the boat and up to the surface.

Once on top, we were suddenly out in these 100 mph winds holding on to these 10 millimetre safety lines on the side of the boat. We had our survival suits on but no life jackets. (Once life jackets are inflated, you can't swim and you can be ballooned away from the boat.) It was completely black and we couldn't see because of the spray.

The first person I saw was John Wills, who came up on the same side of the boat as me. Jon Gornall and Pete were on the other side – but only just. Jon's survival suit had filled with water and he had been seconds from drowning when Pete managed to pull him to the side of the boat, empty his suit and zip him up, thus saving his life.

John Wills had concussion from hitting his head when the roof had ripped off their cabin as the wave struck. He looked shocked, but was holding an EPRIB (Emergency Position Radio Indication Beacon), which was now flashing like a strobe light. Every time the strobe lit up you could see this ashen face. But we knew that rescue must be on its way. The beacon activates automatically when it is submerged in water.

That was when I saw that the *Pink Lady* was in half. It was very sad. It was only connected by lines and stuff.

I got everyone to one side of the boat and then made plans to get the life raft and the 'grab bag' containing the emergency equipment and the satellite phone, which were still in one of the cabins.

Pete Bray, our SAS survivor specialist, said, 'Yep, I'll get that' and dived under the boat into the cabin and got the life raft out. Then he had to dive down a second time to get the grab bag.

When Pete gave me the life raft, a wave hit me and washed me away from the boat. So I'm there with the life raft in my hand thinking, 'Should I let the life raft go or try to swim for it with one arm?'

Suddenly there was a little lull and I was able to swim back to the boat. That was the closest I came to dying. I felt very alone.

All our training and experience told us never to use a life raft. Many people at sea die through going into life rafts – lots of those who died in the Fastnet race were in life rafts. But we had no choice. Our boat was in half. We didn't know how long we would have to wait – it might be twelve hours. So the life raft was our only option.

To inflate the raft in 100 mph winds was the next challenge. You have to pull a line to inflate it. We had done it in training but never in conditions like this. We had two guys holding it while I inflated it. Then I dived in the life raft really quickly to get weight down and we all got in with no problems.

Once in the life raft the big thing for me was saying goodbye to the *Pink Lady*. That boat was my most precious possession after my family. I had invested four years of my life in her and she was worth about £100,000. I just said goodbye, zipped the life raft up and turned to the blokes and said, 'Whatever happens now it doesn't matter – we are safe and alive. We've lost the boat but that doesn't matter.'

The life raft was only one metre square so we were all on top of each other. We took the satellite phone out of the grab bag and then spoke to the coastguard for the first time: 'We're all alive, we are in the lifeboat, *Pink Lady* has gone, we have one casualty with a head injury and one with hypothermia.'

'What's your position?'

I told them our position and they said, 'We've got this telephone number; leave it on and we'll contact you – try and save the batteries.'

Then I called Bob Barnsley, our shore team manager – it was about 2.30 a.m. – and told him what had happened. Bob's unenviable job was to pass on the news to our families.

By now Jon's teeth were chattering and he was white and drifting in and out of sleep. We took his suit off him and wrung it out then put it back on him again. We were all sitting in cold water but we gave him the grab bag to sit on to keep him warm – and huddled around him, making sure we kept him awake.

As we sat in the raft waves broke over us, completely collapsing the raft. You heard this big roar and then a wave hit. Then we had to push all the water out by opening the doors and inflating it. We were in that life raft for six hours. In that time, Jon could have died, but survival is a state of mind and Jon had three guys around him who were strong for him.

We had been told by our control room at Falmouth that a Nimrod [an RAF plane with thirteen crew] had been launched. At around 7.30 a.m., it flew really low over us circling round, flashing lights. The moment we heard it, we put up a flare.

At the same time a 150-metre refrigerated container ship called the *Scandinavian Reefer* diverted fifty miles to come and rescue us. It arrived at about the same time as the Nimrod.

The weather was dropping very slightly but the wind was still gusting at around 60–70 mph and waves were crashing over the front and back of the *Scandinavian Reefer*.

The captain was worried and told the coastguard, 'I don't know if I can rescue them.' He said he would try to pull his boat alongside us to shelter us from the worst of the weather and would pull us aboard if he could.

It was a fantastic piece of seamanship from the skipper, coming alongside us in those conditions. It took him between thirty minutes and an hour. Then they were able to fire a line to us and pull us alongside the boat. Opening up the life raft was difficult. Each time we opened it, the waves broke in – and we were rising and falling at an alarming rate alongside the ship. One minute we were level with the rescuers on the deck, the next minute we were in line with the barnacles underneath the bottom of the boat.

The rescue was the most dangerous part. If one of us fell into the sea we would be swept away and there was little chance of surviving. They threw a fifty-foot rope ladder down and each of us climbed it empowered by adrenaline. Jon went first – Pete was the last. After six hours in the life raft we were rescued.

When I lay on the deck of the boat it was such a lovely feeling to be still. I tried to get up to shake the hands of our rescuers but immediately fell down very hard. I hadn't walked or stood up for thirty-eight days so I didn't know how to walk. My legs were so weak.

So I crawled across the deck towards them. I remember looking up at these six guys – three of them were South American with lovely tanned faces, white teeth and big smiles – and thanking them for saving our lives. We stayed on the ship and arrived in Foynes, Ireland, where the world's media were waiting.

All the major TV stations were there – parliament was out, there was no Olympic Games or football, so they just hooked onto this story about four Britons in a hurricane. Everybody interviewed us. There was something like ten and a half hours of footage on Sky, BBC, ITV . . . it was a global story. Satellite vans were queuing up outside our home with 'live links' from Paula as we got off the ship.

She was talking to Radio Five Live on the radio as she watched us getting off. Then we were flown to Southampton by plane, and Paula and the girls were waiting to meet me there. It wasn't easy as all the TV cameras were filming us. Then we got in the car together to go home.

In the car on the way home from the airport I told Paula that while I was in the boat I'd promised God I was going to do an Alpha course. She said, 'What did you say?'

I said, 'I'll go on an Alpha course.' At that, the girls in the back started cheering and going crazy, 'Yeah! Daddy's going to do an Alpha course!' After what I'd been through, being back with my family brought this overwhelming feeling of love and affection.

A few weeks later, I turned up for the first night of the Alpha course, which was held in somebody's home. There were about twenty people there. After a meal we watched the video. I spent a long time talking about religion and values. Soon after that, I learned that people from the church had been praying for me while I was in the Atlantic. That made me think.

Meanwhile, I wanted to give myself space and time. I had lots of heartfelt questions that I needed answered and Alpha was helping me to explore them. I kept going back week after week – and started going along to the church on Sundays with the family too.

There were two guys on the course who were completely anti-Christian and I sort of sided with them a lot of the time. I was taking the logical view on life really. I couldn't take any leap of faith in terms of opening my heart to God.

Then, while I was on the course, Paula went to Toronto to visit a church there called the Toronto Airport Christian Fellowship. It had become famous for having a powerful ministry and she came back full of her experience.

After she came back we went on a family holiday to Bath to cycle along the canal. While there, we heard that the leaders of the Toronto church, Carol and John Arnott, were going to be speaking at a local church. I was intrigued and went along with Paula and the girls. On our way there I was very anti-Christianity and we all had quite a strong debate. They felt I was being rather negative.

When we got there, Carol Arnott was already speaking and we sat and listened for a while. Then, suddenly, she said, 'Is there anyone here who would like to give their life to the Lord?' At that, something amazing happened. I felt this magnet pulling me up to the front.

I was the only one out of about 1,000 people who went up. When I got there, I spoke to Carol and she led me in a prayer asking God to forgive me my sins and to come into my life. That was 25 October 2004. After saying the prayer I laid down on the floor of the church and for two hours I had this awesome feeling – like being covered in warmth and total happiness. I was incredibly happy and content. It felt like I was almost floating. It was beautiful. After that, I ended up going to church three times while we were in Bath.

Then we came home and I went back to Alpha. I tried to explain to the guys who were so anti-Christianity what had happened to me. Everyone was surprised by the change in me – especially my colleagues at work, who still believe I will change back to my old way of thinking.

Suddenly I started to take in more of the Alpha course. I began to learn – and to enjoy learning. I wasn't sitting on the fence any longer.

We go to church as a family now and my relationship with God is growing every day. I pray every day. It is part of my life. I never prayed before. The great place for me to talk or pray to him is when I am exercising – out in the canoe, on the water, with the sun out – or driving the car.

I pray for guidance – the direction I need to go in. Before, Jesus was just somebody I learned about at school. Now Jesus is by my side. He's somebody I have a relationship with and can talk to. I also read the Bible now – I got *The Message*, which is quite easy to read. Before I took up Christianity I had probably read no more than fifteen books in my life. Now I've got loads – all Christian books.

I have always been a happy person, but God has shown me there is more to life and given me a deep-down assurance that his love is always there. As a Christian family we get more excited about what the future holds for us.

That hurricane got my attention – nothing before had, not even the Falklands. I had my lovely family but there was always something in my heart asking, 'What are we all here for? What is it all about?' God sent me a hurricane.

Now I'm going to let God make the choice about our future.

Mark Stubbs and his family continue to attend their local church in Southampton, where Mark helps with a homeless project.

Alpha is a series of interactive sessions exploring the Christian faith.

Each talk looks at a different question around faith and is designed to create conversation. Alpha is run all around the globe, and everyone's welcome.

It runs in cafés, churches, universities, homes - you name it.

––––––––––

To find out more or to run Alpha, go to
alpha.org

To purchase Alpha resources, go to
shop.alpha.org

Books by Nicky Gumbel

Why Jesus? 'The clearest, best illustrated and most challenging short presentation of Jesus that I know.' – Michael Green

Why Christmas? The Christmas version of *Why Jesus?*

Questions of Life In fifteen compelling chapters Nicky Gumbel points the way to an authentic Christianity that is exciting and relevant to today's world.

Searching Issues The seven issues most often raised by people exploring faith, including suffering, other religions, science and Christianity, and the Trinity.

A Life Worth Living Based on the book of Philippians, this is an invaluable next step for those eager to put their faith on a firm biblical footing.

The Jesus Lifestyle Studies on the Sermon on the Mount showing how Jesus' teaching flies in the face of a modern lifestyle and presents us with a radical alternative.

Bible In One Year

Start your day with the Bible in One Year, a free Bible reading app with commentary by Nicky and Pippa Gumbel from HTB in London.

Nicky Gumbel provides insightful commentary on each Bible passage, intended to be read or listened to alongside the Bible to provide fresh understanding of the texts. Join over 3.5 million users worldwide for this daily Bible reading plan.

Also with NIV audio Bible
from actor David Suchet.

  YouVersion

Subscribe to the daily email:
bibleinoneyear.org

HODDER &
STOUGHTON

Hodder & Stoughton is the UK's
leading Christian publisher,
with a wide range of books from
the bestselling authors in the UK
and around the world ranging from
Christian lifestyle and theology to
apologetics, testimony and fiction.
We also publish the world's
most popular Bible translation
in modern English, the New
International Version, renowned
for its accuracy and readability.

Hodderfaith.com   Hodderbibles.co.uk

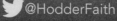 @HodderFaith    /HodderFaith